LIGHTS...
CAMERA...
ARCH!

St. Louis
& the
Movies

By Lester N. Pope

Foreword by
St. Louis
film star

NOTICE TO READERS

Unlike in a movie review, the films covered in this book have their full storylines revealed, with each production's details presented in chronological sequence. Readers who do not wish to know the complete plotlines prior to viewing these films may wish to cease reading midway through the respective chapters. Most of the movies featured in *Lights...Camera...Arch! St. Louis & the Movies* are readily available to borrow from public libraries, to rent from video stores, and to purchase from Internet providers.

Library of Congress Control Number: 2006920812

ISBN: 1-891442-37-6

Book designed by Amy Firestone Rosen.

Edited by Fran Levy.

Virginia Publishing Co.
PO Box 4538
St. Louis, MO 63108
www.stl–books.com

CONTENTS

DEDICATION

To my beautiful and beloved wife, Ruth,
for all her support for everything I do

and

To my multi-talented sons,
of whom I am extremely proud:
Martin — actor, director, playwright, and screenwriter
&
Aaron — script supervisor, director, and screenwriter

and

To my late mother, Ona,
who stirred my interest in reading (and thereafter writing)
because of her insatiable appetite for the printed word

and

To my friend, Rod Lipham,
who encouraged my interest in film and also in writing,
while we were yet children

FOREWORD
Hometown at the Movies

I don't think there's a finer place on Earth than St. Louis, Missouri. It works for me. I'm very comfortable in St. Louis. The people are great, and, if I have my way, I'll live there again some day. I grew up in Affton, I guess one of the first suburbs of south St. Louis County. That's where I lived until I was 18 years old. So, I reckon I'm a real hometown St. Louisan.

I was, I guess, in seventh grade, and I did a play and forgot my dialogue. We were doing a production of *You Can't Take it With You,* and I had a rather long speech, so I got up and decided to make it longer. Because I didn't know what I was doing, I just walked around the table and improvised and sat back down. I was scared to death, but it seemed to work. I had this beautiful acting teacher who gave me a nice big hug and kiss afterward, and I realized, well, there was a nugget here.

Then in high school, I did two spring musicals my junior and senior year. I attended a year at Meramec Community College before I went down to Springfield, Missouri. When I started at Meramec, I really didn't have any idea of what I wanted to do except stay out of Vietnam. So I decided to call myself a theater major, but I couldn't get any plays (I'd actually taken a 'D' in acting class my first semester there). Then, when I went to Southwest Missouri State, I got serious about it. I had a really good teacher there; not that the teachers weren't good before, but this guy was kind of a father figure for me.

After college, I went away to New York, where I lived from 1975 through 1987, and some of my best days were there, like a couple of things I did off-Broadway with some friends. One was a play called *Half a Lifetime* that we did at Manhattan Theatre Club. Another of my favorites came later when I did the film *The Big Lebowski* with the Coen brothers. Altogether, I've done five films with the Coens (*Raising Arizona, Barton Fink, The Hudsucker Proxy,* and *O Brother, Where Art Thou?* are the others), and I feel good about them all.

Actually, I had a pretty good film career going before I started doing the *Roseanne* TV series. But one of the reasons I took *Roseanne* was that I was tired of living out of a suitcase, going from movie to movie.

I've done more than 50 movies and a lot of television shows in the last three decades, and some have been better than others. But it all started for me when I forgot my lines and had to wing it in that school play when I was just a kid in St. Louis.

Any time I get to talk about St. Louis, I get long-winded and emotional. But it's a great town, and *Lights...Cameria...Arch! St. Louis & The Movies* is about films that tell the story of the town — along with some details on us so-called movie celebrities who grew up in and around ol' St. Lou. This book lets you take a close look at St. Louis from a lot of different times and from different angles. I bet most of you didn't know there were so many movies about the old hometown. I know I didn't when Lester asked me to write this. Some of the films in the book date from the early "talkie" era of the 1930s, and they range up through 2005, but they all take place (in full or in part) in our Gateway City.

I hope you enjoy reading about St. Louis half as much as I love talking about it.

John Goodman,
November, 2005

INTRODUCTION
Down the Cinematic Path

I was humbled and extremely flattered when this book's author, Lester N. Pope, asked me if I would write the introduction to his examination of St. Louis and its longstanding relationship with motion pictures.

I have adored movies since I was old enough to be taken to the theater, but not quite yet old enough to behave. The memories of it are a bit dim since it was more than 40 years ago, but my brain can still envision a few short bursts of activity on the afternoon my mother took me to see *Dumbo* at the old Rio Theater at Riverview and West Florissant. The sensations I experienced were overwhelming — a darkened theater with lots of strangers, fistsful of popcorn and candy, loud music, vibrant colors, the supreme heartbreak I felt when the shy little elephant was teased because of his big funny ears, and then suddenly the elation that he could fly! It was glorious. At the age of four, I was officially and completely hooked on the intoxicating power and magic of the moving picture. Television was quickly becoming an integral component of my young life already by that point, but going to the movies was a revered special event. Over the years I recall any number of profound film experiences that I shared with my family and friends, including *The Sting; Young Frankenstein; The Longest Yard; Tommy; Grease; Mary Poppins; Willy Wonka;* and *Chitty Chitty Bang Bang*. These elaborate dances of celluloid, sound, color, and light possessed me and led me down the cinematic path that my life has taken.

We aren't anywhere near Hollywood — about 1800 some-odd miles from my office by car. What St. Louis has, though, is a rich heritage of films that either have taken place in St. Louis or, in some cases, were actually filmed in the metro area — plus a bevy of world-famous actors who hail from my beloved city.

For more than a 100 years, we have marveled at and congratulated ourselves on hosting what is still considered to be the most lavish World's

Fair of all time. Of course, St. Louisans are equally fond of director Vincente Minnelli's *Meet Me in St. Louis*, starring actresses Judy Garland and a young Margaret O'Brien. I'm sure I have seen it at least a dozen times, but my pulse still races when Tootie gets herself into trouble with that bag of flour, and I've been known to not-so-quietly sing along when Esther bares her lovesick soul on that noisy, crowded piece of public transportation. Legend has it that "The Trolley Song" was done on the first take. Thanks for that, Judy! And more than four decades later, St. Louis was seen as an unnamed endless suburbia in director Ron Howard's terrific ensemble film, *Parenthood,* starring Steve Martin. The talented young actor who played Diane Wiest's angst-ridden and overly horny adolescent son, Garry, was Leaf Phoenix, who has since reverted to his birth name of Joaquin. The noisy and neurotic, yet loving, extended circle of relatives portrayed in the film underscores our city's sincere commitment to and love for family.

Long before I knew that people had things called sex and sexualities, I had a fascination with a voluptuous vamp named Mae West. This larger-than-life actress was actually only about 5'3" tall, yet she more than filled any room she entered. Ms. West was a witty, brilliant entertainer and savvy businesswoman with amazing control over her career. She wrote a number of hit plays and nine of the films in which she starred, including *Belle of the Nineties* (a.k.a., *That St. Louis Woman)*. In this, one of her many highly successful feature films, she plays Ruby Carter, a burlesque queen who runs off to New Orleans to get over a man. Of the many randy quotables Ms. West imparted to our culture, I admire this one the most: "I believe in censorship. After all, I made a fortune out of it."

The '50s brought us a triple serving of films with our city's own name in their titles (*The Pride of St. Louis, The Spirit of St. Louis,* and *The Great St. Louis Bank Robbery*). Each of these featured famous and/or infamous individuals who put us all under a great big spotlight because of their actions. To be fair, it's hard to compare the exploits of some thieves to two exalted heroes of aviation and baseball. The fact that a young Steve McQueen was one of the robbers makes it exotic and so ultra-cool, however. Book-ending these three films are two heart-wrenching films about Catholic priests who made a positive difference in the lives of poor newsboys and tough-as-nails gang members (*Fighting Father Dunne* and *The Hoodlum Priest*). Stories such as these are a profound counterpoint to the recent front-page stories of local clergy members' misconduct.

I had a friend, Tommy Gross, who was the biggest movie nut I have ever known. His whole life revolved around films of all types — from big splashy things like *Ghostbusters* and *Raiders of the Lost Ark* to the quiet grace of smaller titles such as *Cross Creek* and *Local Hero*. It was the thrill of his life to work on the local set of *White Palace,* which was written by the late St. Louis writer Glenn Savan and filmed literally all over town. I was so proud to be connected to somebody who was living his dream, making a film in this city. When he died in a tragic accident a few weeks after a few final scenes were lensed in New York, his mother gave me his *White Palace* t-shirt. The colors were already a bit faded, since he had worn it so much, but it became one of my most cherished possessions. I still have it tucked away in my dresser. I also have countless connections to members of the cast, crew, and memorable St. Louis locations. It may not have been the greatest film ever made, but this bittersweet tale of an unexpected, emotional love affair between two lost souls, Nora and Max (Susan Sarandon and James Spader), will always have a special place in my heart and still touches me deeply to this day. I think about that film often.

During part of the spring and summer of 1992, independent filmmaking guru Steven Soderbergh was in our town to direct the superb, deeply textured coming-of-age melodrama, *King of the Hill,* which is based on the memoirs of another St. Louis son — A. E. Hotchner. This lush and tender film was a "four-star" hit with critics and featured up-and-coming actors Jesse Bradford and Adrien Brody. Much of the filming took place in the Central West End, which has been "ground zero" for almost every aspect of my adult social and professional lives. Jeroen Krabbe, Karen Allen, Elizabeth McGovern, and the late Spalding Gray also inhabit this rich vision of Depression-era St. Louis.

Two films discussed in this book reflect a fraction of the richness that the African-American population of St. Louis has contributed to our local culture and history for more than 240 years. Oscar-winning director Taylor Hackford (*Ray, Dolores Claiborne*) celebrated the 60th birthday concert of legendary rock 'n' roll icon Chuck Berry at the Fox Theatre with 1987's *Chuck Berry: Hail! Hail! Rock 'n' Roll.* I wish I could say I was there, but unfortunately I can't. My brother Robb was, however, and he says it was one of the greatest experiences of his life. Berry is widely regarded as one of the undisputed kings of rock 'n' roll. On the other side of the throne room is Tina Turner. Angela Bassett was mesmerizing in 1993's smash hit *What's Love Got To Do With It?* — the brutally honest biography of Turner based on her book *I, Tina.* Ms. Turner may not have been born here, but that powerful, raw voice of hers was. All hail to the king and queen! I have a strong hunch that black stars like Nelly and Cedric the Entertainer, plus Cedric's producer and St. Louis resident Eric Rhone, will soon be making films in or about their hometown, as well — St. Louis style!

In the past eight years or so, two high-profile films were also shot here — *The Big Brass Ring*, directed by fellow St. Louis University High alum and St. Louis native George Hickenlooper (*The Man From Elysian Fields*, *The Mayor of the Sunset Strip*) and, most recently, *The Game of Their Lives*, helmed by award-winning director David Anspaugh (*Hoosiers*, *Rudy*.) Both films brought to town a cast of bona fide movie stars and employed dozens of local actors and crew members. I attended local premiere screenings of both films and the audience could not have been more enthusiastic. Proud St. Louisans cheered equally for their friends and family who were extras and for well-known locations about town. Always polite to strangers, we also applauded the "out-of-town" talent, such as William Hurt, Miranda Richardson, Wes Bentley, and Gerard Butler.

There are a dozen movie stars featured in these pages as well — many of them equally known for their memorable roles on the "small screen" — who either were born and raised here or have strong St. Louis connections. We proudly claim them as our extended movie kin. Five mesmerizing women grace this list: the petite, multi-talented beauty Virginia Mayo (*The Best Years of Our Lives*); celebrated pin-up queen Betty Grable (*How to Marry a Millionaire*); the outrageous and groundbreaking comedienne Phyllis Diller (*Did You Hear the One About the Traveling Saleslady?*); the legendary character actress Agnes Moorehead (*Citizen Kane*); and the searingly intense Oscar winner, Shelley Winters (*A Patch of Blue*, *Lolita*). Esther Williams may have made a career of acting while wet, but she never came close to Belle Rosen's heroic swim in *The Poseidon Adventure*.

The roster of seven men is equally impressive, with their amazing range of styles and particular talents. Classically trained Vincent Price (*The Abominable Dr. Phibes*) is indelibly etched in our minds as a "master of horror," despite his long list of major dramatic roles, including the noir classic *Laura*. He is widely known for his narration of the groundbreaking Michael Jackson music video "Thriller" and the poignant role of the inventor in *Edward Scissorhands*. Long before the silliness of TV's *The Beverly Hillbillies*, actor Buddy Ebsen appeared in *Breakfast at Tiffany's* and dozens of popular Westerns.

Robert Guillaume parlayed a minor role on the wacky and controversial series *Soap* into a full career equally at home on the silver screen and the tube. Similarly, *Quantum Leap* star Scott Bakula acted in between commercials before landing his choice supporting role in Best Picture winner *American Beauty*. It seems like Kevin Kline can be amazing at any role he takes, from his Oscar-winning performance as the ruthless thief in *A Fish Called Wanda* to the morally and emotionally misguided father and husband in *The Ice Storm*. Redd Foxx broke racial ground as a pioneering comedian decades before his penultimate role of Fred Sanford in the hilarious *Sanford and Son*. His film roles were few in number but highly memorable, including *Norman, Is That You?* and *Harlem Nights*. Last but not least is the big man with a huge talent, John Goodman. He will forever be the lovable bear of a husband, Dan Conner, from TV's hit series *Roseanne*, but he continues to challenge himself and his fans with tour-de-force performances in dozens of films such as *The Big Lebowski, Raising Arizona, O Brother, Where Art Thou?* and the voice of sweet-on-the-inside monster Sulley in the animated film *Monsters Inc*. During the enjoyable process of writing this introduction I was able to get a sneak peek at the foreword to this very book written by Mr. Goodman. It made me proud to read how proud he is of his St. Louis roots. I tip my hat and nod my head to you, sir. Let's have a beer sometime!

Now, go make some popcorn, pour a beverage of your choice into an oversized wax cup, and enjoy Lester N. Pope's loving homage to these women, men, and films that help us celebrate who we are and show the world what they are missing by not living in St. Louis.

Chris Clark
Executive Director of Cinema St. Louis
and the St. Louis International Film Festival
December, 2005

Steve Martin filming *Planes, Trains & Automobiles* at Lambert Airport (Courtesy *West End Word*)

AUTHOR'S PREFACE
Before the Features Begin...

So many movies…so little time.

I can't remember when I didn't love movies. I was a really poor kid who grew up on a farm in rural north Georgia. We had a movie theater in my hometown where I remember going a few times when I was very young — then they closed the theater down!

When I was about 10 years old, my father scraped enough money together to get our first TV set, and I discovered a world of movies at my fingertips — on the TV screen! Then I was devastated when Dad died less than two years after we got that TV. I had plenty to do around the farm as I was growing up, but one of the Atlanta stations ran an "Early Show" at 5 o'clock in the afternoon, and I would hurry to get my chores completed so I could check out what was playing on the "boob tube." It was on the "Early Show" that I first saw *The Thing* (with a pre-*Gunsmoke* James Arness as the "Thing"), and it nearly scared me out of my wits. Then there was *Abbott & Costello Meet Frankenstein*, and this time I laughed while being scared, too. In those days, I loved the classic horror flicks — and, well, I guess I still do.

Later, a school friend encouraged my interest in collecting reel-to-reel, 8-mm silent movies, and I bought Chaplin and Laurel & Hardy films any time I could come up with the cash to order them. My home movie projector was one that had to be cranked by hand — I couldn't afford one of those "fancy" kinds with its own motor, but that didn't stop me. I would turn that crank and enjoy every film over and over again.

That same friend (his name is Rod Lipham, by the way, and we're still buddies after all these decades and the hundreds of miles that separate us) is one of the two people most responsible for me becoming a writer. We were both 13 when I told him that I wanted to be a writer, and he offered a very simple response: "If you want to write, read!" Pretty astute for a young teenager in the late '50s, it occurs to me.

The other person most responsible for my choice of careers was my mother, who had only an eighth-grade education, but she loved to read. So I brought her books from the school library, and she devoured them. One of the vivid memories of my childhood is of her sitting, churning with her right hand while reading the book she held in her left.

Okay, hold on! The movies and the writing come together soon….

Because I wanted to be a writer, I decided I needed to go to college. Only one of my six siblings (all several years older) had even finished high school, but I was determined. I had begun writing professionally for my hometown paper when I was 16 after winning three essay contests. I covered high school sporting events to begin with; then they gave me a column all my own during my senior year. Later, I started writing full time during the summer between my junior and senior years at the University of Georgia, and it was at this newspaper that I began my career as a critic. At first, I was reviewing books and plays and movies all, and I couldn't believe that I was getting paid to give my opinions about these! It was like a dream come true. Eventually, I went on to write for several newspapers and magazines, to present reviews on the radio, and to teach writing on the college level, including a course called "Critical Reviewing," in which I shared some of what I'd learned as a critic and, I hope, helped others to focus their own critical skills.

Throughout the years, I've continued to love movies, and I continue to write film reviews for a weekly newspaper, a monthly magazine, and an online Website. Now, with this book, I take a step beyond reviewing — to look at a whole group of motion pictures and the one thing they share in common: All their stories occur partially or completely in St. Louis, Missouri. Some were actually filmed in the Gateway City, while others were made elsewhere but are set in St. Louis. Still, all tell some portion of the story of this first great Mississippi River town.

In *Lights…Camera…Arch! St. Louis & The Movies*, I've done something I always told my Critical Reviewing students never to do in their reviews — divulge the endings of the movies! But these aren't reviews, so I decided to treat these films differently than I do when reviewing a movie. In the pages to follow, you will discover that I attempt to give detailed storylines of each featured film. Before and after these plot summaries, I also offer some of my opinions (after all, I *am* a critic!), but these comments aren't the dominant elements in the chapters. Reviews are something of a "tease" for the reader, designed to pique interest in the item being reviewed. However, information about the movies in this book is more…well, information. It is presented to *inform* readers about these films with St. Louis settings, not simply to pique their interests.

Besides the chapters about St. Louis movies, I'm also providing short biographies of the dozen major motion picture stars with significant St. Louis connections, emphasizing their cinematic accomplishments. And my "intermission" in the middle of the book contains what I hope are "fun facts" about all the films and stars featured.

Finally, I greatly appreciate the contributions of John Goodman and Chris Clark to this effort. Over the years, John has become a "big" star in more ways than one, and he continues to impress us with both his on-screen work and the devotion he feels for his home community. And Chris, as executive director of Cinema St. Louis and the St. Louis International Film Festival, constantly encourages a diversity of cinematic tastes in the hometown that he, likewise, loves.

So, without further ado, here is *Lights...Camera...Arch! St. Louis & the Movies*.

"Quiet on the set...and action!"

Lester N. Pope
December 2005

That St. Louis Woman
(Belle of the Nineties)
1934

Directed by Leo McCarey
Written by Mae West

Primary Cast:

Ruby Carter	*Mae West*
Tiger Kid	*Roger Pryor*
Brooks Claybourne	*Johnny Mack Brown*
Molly Brant	*Katherine DeMille*
Ace Lamont	*John Miljan*
Kirby	*James Donlan*
Dirk	*Stuart Holmes*
Slade	*Harry Woods*
Stogie	*Edward Gargan*
Jasmine	*Libby Taylor*
Colonel Claybourne	*Frederick Burton*
Mrs. Claybourne	*Augusta Anderson*
Blackie	*Benny Baker*
Butch	*Morrie Cohan*
St. Louis Fighter	*Warren Hymer*

When you watch *That St. Louis Woman*, try to maintain a historical perspective. Not only does the story take place more than a century ago, but it has now been more than seven decades since the film itself was produced — just a few short years after the movies found a voice. So try not to judge it from a 21st-century perspective.

Many film buffs are familiar with the name Mae West. Some have even seen her in a few movies, but much about the actress is unknown to modern

audiences. So here are some interesting points to ponder. First, although she lived to be 87 years old, she appeared in only 13 motion pictures, 10 of those in the 1930s and '40s. Next, consider that she began her film career at a time when even the mention of sex was largely taboo, yet she became known as a woman who flaunted her sexuality. Finally, it's likely that few today realize that many of those classic movie lines that came from her mouth also came from her mind. She was actually the writer of nine of the 13 movies she appeared in, including *That St. Louis Woman*.

This is the story of beauty queen/singer, Ruby Carter (Mae West). As the film opens, patrons (mainly men) are filing into a show hall under a banner that proclaims: "Here! Here! Here! Ruby Carter — the Most Talked About Woman in America."

Inside the theater, we see a troupe of leotard-clad dancers performing a song from the Gay Nineties. The first thing we notice about these women is that they are much larger and more curvaceous and voluptuous than would be (the standard for) dancers of later years, and the song they are performing seems corny by later standards.

Then Ruby Carter is introduced with glowing remarks. When the curtain opens each of several times, she's simply dressed in different costumes, but the audience of men goes wild.

Some time after the show, we see a carriage pull up in front of a home, and Ruby disembarks along with the boxing contender, Tiger Kid (Roger Pryor). But the couple is stopped by Tiger's manager, Kirby (James Donlan), as they are about to go inside. He tries to prevent his boxer from accompanying Ruby, but both Tiger and Ruby ignore Kirby, even as the manager insists he's not leaving until Tiger does.

They sit around her place, with Tiger telling Ruby how much he loves her. When it starts to rain, Tiger gets concerned about Kirby, so Ruby suggests he throw an umbrella out the window to the other man. While he's doing that, Ruby slips over to the phone and calls the police, asking them to pick up the "suspicious" man outside her home.

It becomes readily obvious that Tiger is extremely jealous of Ruby and other men. Even looking at photos of her with others she's known before they met gets him upset. His insecurity shows in his conversation with his performer girlfriend.

In the next scene, Kirby is in the gym, where he has set up a scene to make Tiger think that Ruby is two-timing him. The boxer "overhears" another man call Ruby and make a date. Afterward, Tiger writes a letter to her, telling her how badly she has treated him.

Afterward, Ruby's manager convinces her it's time to get out of St. Louis for a while and take her act on the road, proposing that she go to New Orleans. Considering how her relationship with Tiger has turned out, she decides to take the suggestion.

When her riverboat arrives, the St. Louis woman is met with a string of admirers down South. She is to perform and stay at Ace Lamont's Sensation House while in New Orleans, and Ace himself makes advances toward Ruby right away, but she puts him off. She seems more impressed by one of the club's frequent attendees, Brooks Claybourne (Johnny Mack Brown).

As time goes by, we see flocks of men hovering around Ruby, but no one seems to be close to her as Tiger was. Claybourne sends her expensive diamond necklaces and bracelets, but the two of them never seem to be alone together.

Not only does Ace Lamont (John Miljan) own Sensation House, but he seems to be a boxing promoter, as well. He has a fight scheduled against the champ, but Ace's contender seems to have left town. Now Ace is faced with having to pay the champ's fee whether or not he fights, so he decides to find a replacement. At a local gym, he sees a boxer who's just arrived in town — a boxer whom he thinks could even beat the champ. That boxer is, of course, Tiger Kid. Ace offers Tiger a "shot" at the title if does him a small favor. He says that he's bought a lot of jewelry for a woman, and he wants Tiger to steal it back for him.

That evening, Ace is taking Ruby for a carriage ride down by the river when they are accosted, and the thief makes off with Ruby's diamonds, given to her by Brooks Claybourne.

Later, Ruby sees Tiger talking to Ace at Sensation House, and she snoops as Ace stashes her jewelry in his safe. That's when she decides to get even with both men. She gets word to Brooks to bet against Tiger in the upcoming fight, knowing that Ace has bet heavily on her ex-boyfriend to defeat the champ.

At the boxing bout, unlike modern fights that go a specified number of rounds, Ace and Ruby are at ringside as the match goes into the 27th round without a winner. As Ace is watching the action, Ruby spikes Tiger's water bottle, which Ace hands to his boxer, not knowing he's sealing his fighter's certain loss.

Back at his club after the match ends in Tiger's defeat, Ace is met by many of his creditors, to whom he offers drinks, and says he's going upstairs to get their money.

In the meantime, when Tiger approaches Ruby again, she tells him that she knows he was the man who robbed her. Tiger readily admits his crime but says he thought the woman whose jewelry he stole in the dark was Ace's former girlfriend, Molly.

When Ace goes for the stolen jewelry, he discovers that it's missing from his safe — retrieved by Ruby, who watched him open it and jotted down the combination. So the club owner decides the best thing for him is to burn down Sensation House and clear out. Before he goes, he grabs Molly (Katherine DeMille) and locks her in his office closet. Then he douses the place with kerosene.

Before Ace can make good his get-away, Tiger confronts him, and Ace pulls a gun on the boxer. But Tiger knocks him down before he can shoot. When he checks the other man, Tiger discovers that he has killed the club owner. When he tells Ruby what he's done, she reassures him. Then the couple hears shouts from the closet, and they rescue Molly.

At the conclusion of the film, we see a number of headlines about Tiger turning himself in and being acquitted of manslaughter, having killed Ace in self-defense. Then, in the final scene, we see Ruby and Tiger getting married.

This movie has had a number of (working) titles. Variously known as the *Belle of St. Louis*, *Belle of New Orleans*, *It Ain't No Sin*, and *It Isn't Any Sin*, the most widely used title is *Belle of the Nineties*.

There are a number of songs throughout this film, most of them sung by Mae West in the style of the 19th century — so *That St. Louis Woman* could be considered a musical. Perhaps the best of these songs is "I'm Gonna Drown Down in Those Troubled Waters," which Mae sings when she overhears an outdoor prayer meeting that her maid, Jasmine (Libby Taylor), is attending.

Granted, this production is nothing like movies being made in the 21st century, but it demonstrates a lot of character not typical of films of that period. First of all, the story was written by a woman, Mae West herself, and it's filled with the sexual innuendos that typically pervaded her movies in defiance of the more Puritanical ethic of that time period. And, more significantly, Mae created a strong woman as the lead character, not some "damsel in distress" who had to be rescued by a man, as was the norm for movies of the 1930s. No, Mae's Ruby Carter, was fully in charge, and few who've seen *That St. Louis Woman* could doubt it.

STAR

Agnes Moorehead
Born December 6, 1900

Agnes Moorehead's real "bewitching" power was to make you believe in the character she was portraying, whether in film or on the small screen.

Although not born in St. Louis (she began her life in Clinton, Massachusetts), Agnes came to the Gateway City as a child, when she got her start in theater, dancing and performing on stage. She was featured on the radio at age 23, when that new contraption was just finding its way into American culture.

Deciding she wanted to concentrate on her career as a performer, Agnes relocated to New York City, where she appeared on Broadway and continued her love of broadcast by joining Orson Welles' Mercury Theater ensemble. Her film debut also came with this same group in 1941, and what a debut it was! She played Mary Kane in Welles' famous *Citizen Kane*, considered by many critics to be the greatest American film ever made.

Other motion pictures followed quickly for Agnes, including *The Magnificent Ambersons* (for which she received her first Oscar nomination) and *The Big Street*, both in 1942. Then there was *Journey Into Fear*, *The Youngest Profession*, and *Government Girl*, all in 1943, followed by *Jane Eyre*, *Since You Went Away*, *The Seventh Cross*, *Mrs. Parkington*, and *Tomorrow the World* in 1944. The next year, she appeared in *Keep Your Powder Dry*, *Her Highness and the Bellboy*, and *Our Vines Have Tender Grapes*.

The second half of the 1940s saw Agnes in *Dark Passage*; *The Lost Moment*; *Summer Holiday*; *The Woman in White*; *Station West*; *Johnny Belinda*; *The Stratton Story*; *The Great Sinner*; and *Without Honor*.

Entering her fifties, Agnes graced the screen in 15 films during the next five years: *Black Jack*; *Caged*; *Fourteen Hours*; *Adventures of Captain Fabian*; *Show Boat*; *The Blue Veil*; *The Blazing Forest*; *The Story of Three Loves*; *Scandal at Scourie*; *Main Street to Broadway*; *Those Redheads from Seattle*; *Magnificent*

Agnes Moorehead (from the *Globe-Democrat* Collection at the St. Louis Mercantile Library, University of Missouri–St. Louis)

Obsession; Untamed; The Left Hand of God; and *All That Heaven Allows.*

Agnes didn't slow her pace much during the second half of the 1950s, during which she performed in 13 movies: *The Conqueror; Meet Me in Las Vegas; The Swan; The Revolt of Mamie Stover; Pardners; The Opposite Sex; The True Story of Jesse James; Jeanne Eagels; Raintree County; The Story of Mankind; Tempest; Night of the Quarter Moon;* and *The Bat.*

Finally, going into her sixties, Agnes began to slow her pace, but she continued to do many fine films that are now considered classics. Between 1960 and 1964, she appeared in eight productions: *Pollyanna; Twenty Plus Two; Bachelor in Paradise; Jessica; Poor Mr. Campbell; How the West Was Won; Hush...Hush Sweet Charlotte;* and *Who's Minding the Store?*

In 1964, Agnes Moorehead made a slight turn in her career, taking a recurring role on a television series — although she had previously appeared in "guest" roles on such anthology programs as *The Twilight Zone.* That year, she took on the part of Endora on the series *Bewitched,* and the show continued on the air for a full eight years (which surprised Agnes, who had thought the show would last a single year, at the most).

Although she is enshrined in many memories as *Bewitched's* Endora, the mother of the main character of the story, it is said that Agnes really didn't like making the show because she had to get up before 5:00 a.m. in order to get to makeup by 6 o'clock, and filming often went on until 8:00 in the evening.

Even while *Bewitched* was in production, she continued her motion picture career, appearing in eight films between 1964 and 1972: *The Singing Nun; Alice Through the Looking Glass; The Ballad of Andy Crocker; The Strange Monster of Strawberry Cove; What's the Matter with Helen; Marriage: Year One; Suddenly Single; Rolling Man;* and *Night of Terror.*

After *Bewitched,* she was the voice of the Goose in the *Charlotte's Web* animated film in 1973, and she appeared in two television productions that year and the next: *Frankenstein: The True Story* and *Rex Harrison Presents Stories of Love.* She died on April 30, 1974, in Rochester, Minnesota, but she was featured one final time on the large screen in the ironically titled *Dear Dead Delilah,* released in 1975.

One of the films that she appeared in was *The Conqueror* (released in 1956), which was filmed two years earlier in the Nevada desert, near where the U.S. government was engaged in nuclear tests. Several of that production's stars subsequently died of cancer, including Agnes Moorehead, John Wayne, Dick Powell, Susan Hayward, and Pedro Armendariz, and some people feel that there is a link between the tests and those deaths.

Agnes Moorehead was nominated for four Oscars and was the recipient of two Golden Globe Awards and one National Board of Review Award for her work.

Meet Me in St. Louis
1944

Directed by Vincente Minnelli

Written by Sally Benson (novel), Irving Brecher, and Fred F. Finklehoffe

Primary Cast:

Esther Smith	*Judy Garland*
Tootie Smith	*Margaret O'Brien*
Anna Smith	*Mary Astor*
Rose Smith	*Lucille Bremer*
Alonzo Smith	*Leon Ames*
Lon Smith	*Henry H. Daniels, Jr.*
Agnes Smith	*Joan Carroll*
Grandpa	*Harry Davenport*
John Truett	*Tom Drake*
Katie	*Marjorie Main*
Lucille Ballard	*June Lockhart*
Colonel Darly	*Hugh Marlowe*
Warren Sheffield	*Robert Sully*
Mr. Neely	*Chill Wills*

When we think of movies about St. Louis, this is the one that probably comes to mind first. The Judy Garland classic *Meet Me in St. Louis* has all the hallmarks that made it a 1940s success.

Musicals were big in those days, and Judy Garland was a very big singing star. Moviegoers had already seen her in such productions as *The*

MGM's GLORIOUS LOVE STORY WITH MUSIC

MEET ME IN ST. LOUIS

STARRING

Judy GARLAND

WITH *Margaret* O'BRIEN

MARY ASTOR · LUCILLE BREMER
TOM DRAKE · MARJORIE MAIN

Photographed in TECHNICOLOR

SCREEN PLAY BY IRVING BRECHER AND FRED F. FINKLEHOFFE
BASED ON THE BOOK BY SALLY BENSON
A METRO-GOLDWYN-MAYER PICTURE
DIRECTED BY VINCENTE MINNELLI
PRODUCED BY ARTHUR FREED

Wizard of Oz, For Me and My Gal, Ziegfeld Girl, Strike Up the Band, Everybody Sing, and the enormously popular Andy Hardy films, in which she co-starred with Mickey Rooney — so they were ready for another enjoyable outing watching Judy belt out one melodious song after another.

    Meet Me in St. Louis opens with a brief introduction of the primary characters, several of whom, during the early moments of the film, sing portions of that memorable title song:

> *When Louie came home to the flat,*
>
> *He hung up his coat and his hat.*
>
> *He gazed all around, but no wifey he found,*
>
> *So he said, "Where can Flossie be at?"*
> *A note on the table he spied,*
>
> *He read it just once, then he cried.*
>
> *It ran, "Louie dear, it's too slow for me here,*
>
> *So I think I will go for a ride."*

> *"Meet me in St. Louie, Louie,*
>
> *Meet me at the fair.*
> *Don't tell me the lights are shining*
>
> *any place but there.*
> *We will dance the Hoochee Koochee;*
>
> *I will be your tootsie wootsie.*
> *If you will meet in St. Louie, Louie,*
>
> *Meet me at the fair."*

> *The dresses that hung in the hall,*
>
> *Were gone; she had taken them all.*
> *She took all his rings and the rest of his things;*
>
> *The picture he missed from the wall.*
> *"What! moving!" the janitor said,*
>
> *"Your rent is paid three months ahead."*

"What good is the flat?" said poor Louie, "Read that."
And the janitor smiled as he read.

"Meet me in St. Louie, Louie,
Meet me at the fair.
Don't tell me the lights are shining
any place but there.
We will dance the Hoochee Koochee;
I will be your tootsie wootsie.
If you will meet in St. Louie, Louie,
Meet me at the fair."

It's the summer of 1903, and Katie, the maid (Marjorie Main), is busy making a "batch" of ketchup (things like that were all made at home during those days). Also present in the kitchen is the missus of the house, Anna (Mary Astor). Then in comes young daughter, Agnes (Joan Carroll), wearing her soaked long underwear; she obviously has been swimming or playing in the water in back of the affluent Smith home in what would be the suburbs these days. Everybody keeps tasting the ketchup, offering opinions about whether it's too sweet, too sour, or "flat."

As Agnes leaves the room and marches up the grand staircase, she bursts into her rendition of "Meet Me in St. Louis." Knocking on the bathroom door, Agnes is answered by Grandpa (Harry Davenport), who is, likewise, belting out the song. From outside the house, we can hear a chorus of others also singing the title song, and the camera cuts to an overhead view of Esther (Judy Garland) and her friends driving up in a horse-drawn carriage, all singing, "Meet Me in St. Louie, Louie...."

This opening scene sets the stage for the rest of the production.

When Esther enters the kitchen, she, of course, also tastes the ketchup and offers her opinion, then whispers something to Katie while her mother's back is turned; the maid then asks if she can serve dinner an hour early. At first, Anna puts Katie off, saying that Mr. Smith, her husband, doesn't like to eat early on hot days, but when Katie says that she needs to visit her sister who's having "man problems," Anna reluctantly agrees. "But you'll have to explain it to Mr. Smith," she tells Katie.

So what's all this commotion about, anyway? Katie really wants to know why Esther is requesting that dinner be served so early. After all, she had to tell the missus a "flock of lies" to get her to agree to having dinner before its normal time. It's just that Esther's older sister Rose (Lucille Bremer) is expecting a long-distance call from Warren Sheffield (Robert Sully), who is all the way across the country in New York City, and Esther doesn't want Rose to have to talk to Warren in front of the whole family (since, in those days, having a phone at all was a tremendous luxury, and no one had more than one in the house). Esther explains to Katie that she wants Rose to feel like she can say the things to Warren that will elicit a proposal (since, also in those days, daughters were expected to marry in birth order, and, as Rose is the oldest, Esther, who is the second daughter, wants to get her sister "hitched" as soon as possible).

Still, the best-laid plans sometimes go astray, for when the father comes home, he nixes the whole plan of eating dinner an hour early. But I'm getting ahead of the storyline. While the family is waiting for Alonzo to arrive, Rose comes in and hurriedly points out to Esther that their very eligible new next-door neighbor, John Truett (Tom Drake), is standing out in his front yard. So the two young women stroll out onto their front porch and begin speaking loudly to each other in easy earshot of John; but they are totally ignored, as he turns around and goes into his house. Of course, two intelligent young women such as Rose and Esther Smith have other ways of accomplishing their goals. They decide to simply invite John over to their house for a going-away party for their brother Lon (Henry H. Daniels, Jr.), who is about to leave for college.

When Alonzo (Leon Ames) does arrive home from a hard day of practicing law, he announces that he plans to take a bath and cool off and that dinner will be at its normal time. It seems that everyone except Alonzo (including the mother, Anna) knows about the upcoming phone call from New York, and when it does occur, the whole family turns around and listens to the whole conversation between Rose and Warren, which turns out to be a disappointing fizzle, with Warren never once mentioning the subject of marriage.

At the party, we get to know a little bit about the very precocious Tootie Smith (Margaret O'Brien), who is only five. She and Agnes are caught snooping from the stairwell, and those attending the get-together are enchanted with her. Eventually, she ends up singing a very entertaining version of "Under the Bamboo Tree" with Esther. And it seems that Rose and Esther's plans to get John Truett's attention work this time. He attends their party and apparently has a good time. But everyone else starts to depart, and John just cannot find his hat (and, of course, a man at the turn of the 20th century had to have his hat). Finally, Esther "finds" the missing headgear (where she had hidden it earlier) and returns it. Now, with only John and Esther left in the lower portion of the house, she asks John to escort her around as she turns off all the gas lights. Before he realizes it, John is totally smitten with Esther Smith.

Broken into four basic scenes (the four seasons), Meet Me in St. Louis now takes us to Fall, where the two younger Smith children, Agnes and Tootie, are preparing for Halloween. After watching the Halloween scenes, it's easy to understand why the young Margaret O'Brien was such a sought-after child star. Also in one of the Halloween scenes, in a uncredited speaking cameo role, is Darryl Hickman, who four years later would go on to be one of the main stars in another fact-based film likewise set in St. Louis during the early days of the 20th century, Fighting Father Dunne.

It is on Halloween night that Tootie screams, and Esther comes running up to the house with her injured baby sister. While the family is waiting for the doctor to arrive, Tootie makes the assertion that her injury came from being struck by Esther's beau, John Truett. At first, Esther can't believe Tootie and calls her a little liar. Then she decides her sister is telling the truth, so she runs next door and begins to slap and kick and bite John. Later, back at home, Esther discovers that, in fact, Tootie has lied, and John was simply trying to restrain Tootie and Agnes when the two young Smith daughters were trying to plant an obstruction to derail the trolley. So now it's necessary for Esther to again visit John, this time to apologize for her behavior. Of course, he forgives her, grabs her, and gives her the first kiss that the two share.

Later that evening, Alonzo comes in to announce that his law firm is transferring him to New York in January to run the company office there. But this news is definitely not received well by the various members of the Smith household, who would much rather remain in their native St. Louis.

Now the film jumps ahead to Christmastime, and Esther is set to go to her last dance in St. Louis with John, but Rose doesn't have a date for the occasion. Warren Sheffield is bringing another girl, Lucille Ballard (June

A scene from *Meet Me in St. Louis* (MPTV.net)

A scene from *Meet Me in St. Louis* (Courtesy *West End Word*)

Lockhart), so she reluctantly agrees to attend the dance with her brother, Lon. While Esther is getting ready for the dance, John shows up at the back door to tell her that his tuxedo is at the cleaners, which closed before he could pick it up, so now he can't take her to the dance. After John leaves, a despondent Esther is consoled by her grandfather, who asks if he can take her to the dance instead. At the party, Rose and Esther connive to fill Lucille's dance card with the worst partners available. But, when they meet Lucille, she turns out to be a very charming young woman who proposes that Warren should escort Rose and that she'll be with Lon — leaving Esther with the awkward dance partners she's picked for Lucille (and this turns out to be one of the funniest scenes in the film). Finally, Grandpa feels sorry for Esther and cuts in, dancing her behind the Christmas tree and into John Truett's waiting arms; he has somehow found a way to get his tux and is appropriately clad.

After the dance, standing against a tree in her front yard, John proposes to Esther, asking her not to go to New York but to stay in St. Louis and marry him. But she tells him that he should finish college and that, although she's going to New York with her family, they'll find a way to be together.

Inside her house, she finds Tootie waiting up for Santa, and the youngest Smith isn't looking forward at all to the move that's coming up in a few days. Esther hugs her little sister, but after she sits holding Tootie while singing "Have Yourself a Merry Little Christmas," her sister jumps up and runs outside, crying while knocking over her snow characters with a stick and yelling that if she can't have them, no one else will ever have her snow people. Inside the house, their father is watching the whole scene transpiring outside as Esther runs out to get her sister. That's when Alonzo makes a decision. He calls his whole family out of their beds on Christmas Eve night to announce that they're not moving to New York, that they will stay in St. Louis, and his company will just have to accept his decision.

Now for the Spring scene, in which the whole family leaves for the 1904 World's Fair. As they stand around taking in its grandeur, Esther turns to John in the closing scene and observes: "I can't believe it. Right here where we live — right here in St. Louis!"

But that's just the storyline for this movie, which is only half of it, since this is a musical production from the heyday of Hollywood musicals. The other half is composed of the presentation of those beautiful and melodious numbers. Besides the title tune, among other songs included are: "The Trolley

Song" (which won an Oscar), "The Boy Next Door," "Skip to My Lou," "Under the Bamboo Tree," "You and I," and, of course, "Have Yourself a Merry Little Christmas."

Most people know that this production was built around the excitement about the coming 1904 St. Louis World's Fair, but they generally believe that the characters in this film are entirely fictitious. Not so. In fact, the film *Meet Me in St. Louis* is based on the memoir of Sally Benson that appeared in *The New Yorker* magazine in the early '40s, a memoir that related fond stories of her childhood, growing up in an affluent St. Louis family at 5135 Kensington Avenue around the turn of the 20th century.

It's said that Judy Garland wasn't particularly fond of the idea of co-starring with Margaret O'Brien in this film. The young actress — who, by the way, did get second billing to Garland — had a way of stealing the show in any movie she appeared in, and Judy didn't want to see her movie become young Margaret's story, instead. But Judy did go through with performing in the lead role, and very successfully, too. I dare say, though most will probably readily remember Margaret's performance, no one is likely to think of this as anything other than "a Judy Garland film."

And although we may not see much that reminds us of the ol' home town in *Meet Me in St. Louis* — after all, this story takes place more than a century ago, when Forest Park was "way out west" — it still touches on one of the great adventures in St. Louis' history, the 1904 World's Fair, probably the greatest such undertaking up to that time. And that was a period when St. Louis was one the five largest cities in the nation. The 1904 Louisiana Purchase Exposition (the Fair's real name) is definitely one event I truly wish I had been around to attend.

Overall, *Meet Me in St. Louis* has stood the test of time well. St. Louisans should take great pride that this film, set in their own home town, was chosen by *Time* magazine's critics as one of the 100 best American movies ever made. It's still a joyous adventure to watch this story over and over again, and many of us will inevitably sing along when the film's cast members are performing that catchy title song. .

Buddy Ebsen
Born April 8, 1908

He came to be known the world over as Jed Clampett for his role in the long-running (1962-71) television series, *The Beverly Hillbillies*, but Buddy Ebsen had been a film actor for more than two decades before that show debuted, and his career continued for another two decades after the series ended its run.

Born in the metropolitan St. Louis town of Belleville, Illinois, he lived to be 95, passing away on July 6, 2003, in Torrance, California. His birth name was Christian Rudolph Ebsen, Jr.

His father had owned a dance studio in Belleville and insisted that his son study dancing. So it was natural that Buddy would begin his professional career in the late 1920s as a Broadway chorus dancer, later creating a vaudeville act with his sister, Vilma. The two came to Hollywood to perform in *Broadway Melody of 1936*, which starred Eleanor Powell. After that, his sister left the act and retired from performing while Buddy and his dancing feet went on to do nine other productions in the '30s. These included *Born to Dance*; *Banjo on My Knee*; *Broadway Melody of 1938*; *My Lucky Star*; *Four Girls in White*; and *The Kid from Texas*.

One role that Buddy was scheduled to play never happened. He was originally cast as the scarecrow in *The Wizard of Oz*. Then he exchanged roles with Ray Bolger and was to play the Tin Woodman; but the aluminum dust in the makeup made him ill, so Jack Haley took over the role before the filming began.

In the 1940s, Buddy concentrated on his stage career and appeared in only three films: *They Met in Argentina*, *Parachute Battalion*, and *Sing Your Troubles Away*. Then, in the early 1950s, he made seven films, mostly westerns (*Under Mexicali Stars*; *Silver City Bonanza*; *Thunder in God's Country*; *Rodeo King and the Senorita*; *Utah Wagon Train*, *Night People*; and *Red Garters*) before he was chosen to play Davy Crockett's sidekick, George Russel, in the 1954

Buddy Ebsen (from the *Globe-Democrat* Collection at the St.Louis Mercantile Library, University of Missouri–St. Louis)

Disney television mini-series and subsequent 1956 theatrical film, *Davy Crockett and the River Pirates*. Other film appearances of that period included *Attack* and *Between Heaven and Hell* (both released the same year as the Davy Crockett film).

Buddy seemed to be in a bit of a pattern with his television/movie roles during the '50s. In 1958, he created the role of Sergeant Hunk Marriner in the short-lived TV series *Northwest Passage*, and played the part again in the films *Mission of Danger and Frontier Rangers* (both released in 1959). Then he was Hunk Marriner once more in 1961's *Fury River*. (Actually, these three films were basically re-edits from the 1958 TV series.)

Some will remember Buddy for his portrayal of Doc Golightly in 1961's *Breakfast at Tiffany's*, which starred Audrey Hepburn. The next year, he got his "big break" as TV's Jed Clampett, a gig that lasted nine years. Still, he made a few films during this period, including 1962's *The Interns*, 1964's *Mail Order Bride*, and 1968's *The One and Only, Genuine*, and *Original Family Band*, as well as the TV movie, *The Andersonville Trial*, in 1970.

Buddy wasn't away from television long, only a couple of years, before he began another long-running series, *Barnaby Jones*, which was on the air from 1973 through 1980. During that two-year gap, he appeared in the TV films, *The Daughters of Joshua Cabe* in 1972 and *The Horror at 37,000 Feet*, *Adventures of Tom Sawyer*, and *The President's Plane is Missing* (all three in 1973).

All the rest of Buddy's movie roles were on television except for the last one, 10 years before his death, when he had a cameo role in a theatrical film based on his earlier TV series. While playing Barnaby Jones, he appeared in the TV films, *Smash-Up on Interstate 5*, *Leave Yesterday Behind*, *The Critical List*, and *The Paradise Connection*. He also appeared in the 1978 mini-series, *The Bastard*.

In the 1980s, Buddy appeared in the TV films, *The Return of the Beverly Hillbillies*, *Fire on the Mountain*, and *Stone Fox*. In 1990, he had a role in the TV film, *Working Tra$h*.

Buddy's last film appearance was a good one to go out on, even though it was a bit part. In a nod to both of his hit television series, he again played detective Barnaby Jones, who is hired by Jed Clampett (portrayed by Jim Varney) in the search for the missing Granny in the theatrical version of *The Beverly Hillbillies*.

Although he is known for his work as a performer, Buddy Ebsen wrote six plays, five of which were produced, including a farce called *Honest John* in 1948 and *Champagne General*, a Civil War drama, in 1973. His romantic novel, *Kelly's Quest*, was published in 2001, when he was 93 years old! He died two years later, on July 6, 2003, in Torrance, California.

Fighting Father Dunne
1948

Directed by Ted Tetzlaff

Written by Frank Davis, Martin Rackin, and William Rankin

Primary Cast:

Father Peter Dunne	Pat O'Brien
Matt Davis	Darryl Hickman
Emmett Mulvey	Charles Kemper
Kate Mulvey	Ruth Donnelly
Miss O'Rourke	Una O'Connor
Michael O'Donnell	Arthur Shields
Thomas Lee	Harry Shannon
Steve Davis	Joe Sawyer
Mrs. Knudson	Anna Q. Nilsson
Jimmy	Donn Gift
Paula Hendricks	Myrna Dell
Danny Briggs	Jim Nolan
Tony	Billy Cummings
Chip	Billy Gray
Monk	Eric Roberts
Lefty	Gene Collins
J.J. Sonin	Jason Robards, Sr.
Archbishop Glennon	Lester Matthews

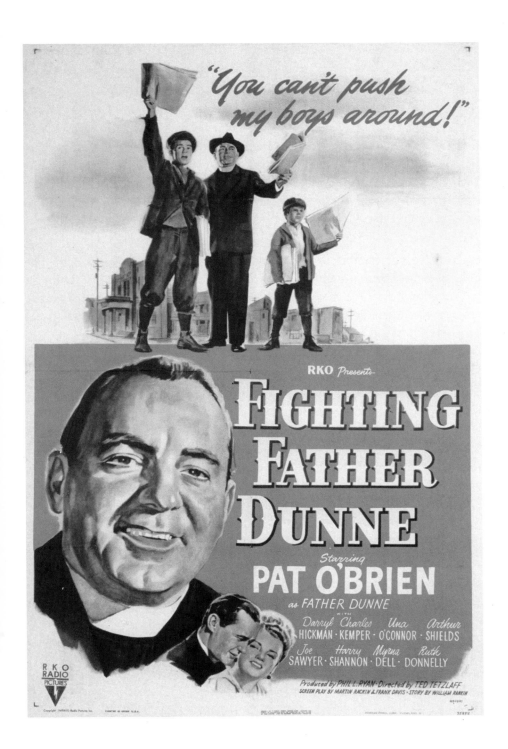

Fighting Father Dunne is set in the same time period as *Meet Me in St. Louis*, and both are centered around actual events, but the stories occur worlds apart.

It's 1905, and the World's Fair has just ended, but many of the characters in this story may not have even been aware of the events that had just unfolded way out at the edge of the city in Forest Park. The primary players in *Fighting Father Dunne* are newsboys, the poorest of the poor, many without parents and without homes, living in the streets and scrapping just to stay alive. This is the true account of a priest who went to bat for these boys to give them a place to live with loving and compassionate caregivers.

"This is the story about a man who lived in St. Louis," read the opening lines of the film. "It is also a tribute to him and what he stood for. The conditions that Father Dunne helped alleviate no longer exist in St. Louis, or in any other city. Today, an enlightened newspaper management all over the country has created a sound opportunity and real security for the newspaper boy."

This story develops in flashback form: It's the 1940s and Father Dunne's Newsboys' Home and Protectorate is about to be demolished. A car stops, and a middle-aged man steps out and asks those tearing down the place if he can have a slab of concrete from in front of the building that is embedded with two footprints — one set a man's, and the other, a boy's. Then we are whizzed back to 1905, and we are introduced to the newsboys of yesteryear, a time when most of the youth selling papers on street corners lived in poverty and were often homeless, staying the night wherever they could find shelter. These poor boys who deliver the papers are huddled around an open street fire waiting for their papers to arrive. When they do, the boys must pay up front to get these papers.

Two boys hitch a ride on the paper wagon but, when discovered, they are kicked off. The same two boys show up a little later at Father Dunne's residence to sell him his daily paper. The priest asks about Chip, his regular paper boy, and one of the boys explains that he is Jimmy (Donn Gift), Chip's brother, and that Chip (Billy Gray, later in *Father Knows Best*) is sick. That's when Father Dunne (Pat O'Brien) decides to check on the sick child. They find him shivering in a cold, makeshift shelter. Father Dunne wraps him in his coat and takes him and the two other boys to his sister's house. The sister (Ruth Donnelly) readily takes the boys in while Father Dunne locates the doctor, who determines that all three youths need to be kept warm and inside. When Father Dunne's brother-in-law, Emmett (Charles Kemper), comes home, he is a little bit annoyed to find three shabby boys sleeping in his bed. But when Father Dunne speaks with Emmett, it's obvious that the other man has a good heart.

The priest goes to Archbishop Glennon (Lester Matthews), seeking funds to open a home for wayward newspaper boys, but the archbishop (whose name — Cardinal Glennon — is now familiar to St. Louisans for the hospital bearing his name) says there is no money to spare. He does eventually give Father Dunne permission to open such a home, but he'll have to find the funds to run it.

Emmett is only too glad to give Father Dunne and the three boys a ride on his brewery wagon to look for a house. After they locate one, the priest goes to find food. At a market run by Mrs. Knudson (Anna Q. Nilsson), he selects some vegetables, but then explains that he has no funds. She's very angry at Father Dunne until he tells her it's for poor newspaper boys; then she graciously contributes everything he wants and more. Unfortunately, it seems that the priest isn't a very good cook, but the poor, hungry boys eat his food anyway.

Next, Father Dunne goes to see the attorney who represents the archdiocese and convinces him to pay the rent for the home. When a pony cart is stolen by two boys, the priest takes charge of the boys and drives the pony cart to its owner. He then gets the man to turn it over to the newspaper boys' home for their use. He later convinces a furniture store owner to donate beds for all his boys, and the man explains that he has three salesmen, and he'd gladly trade all three for Father Dunne if he ever wanted to go to work for him. When Mrs. O'Rourke, a nosy neighbor from across the street, shows up, the priest talks her into volunteering her time as housekeeper and cook.

Then Father Dunne meets his biggest challenge in the form of a boy named Matt Davis (Darryl Hickman, who gets second billing in this film and who had a cameo role in *Meet Me in St. Louis* four years earlier). Matt's character always seems to be a little shady and not quite trustworthy.

The priest and his brother-in-law go to see the editor of the *St. Louis Sun* about the way his boys are being kicked off the best street corners by some of the paper's grown circulation bullies, but it seems to have little effect. Some time later, Matt gets the idea of using the pony cart to help the boys carry their papers around, but they are attacked by the bullies from the *Sun*. The pony, Nubbins, is killed, and Billy is injured. That's when Father Dunne calls the owner of the pony and cart, Michael O'Donnell (Arthur Shields), whereupon O'Donnell calls the *St. Louis Sun* and points out he owns the newspaper's building, and he wants the attacks on the boys to stop.

But Matt, feeling guilty because of Jimmy's injury and Nubbins' death, has gone back to live with his father, who has now been released from jail. Father Dunne calls on Matt and asks him to come back to the home, but the senior Davis tells him his son doesn't want to leave. After the priest is gone, the father beats his son.

Father Dunne decides he has outgrown the house — that there are just too many boys to fit in the space, so he puts together a dinner (that doesn't go quite as planned) to convince community leaders to fund his newspaper boys' home. But only the archdiocese's lawyer and Mr. O'Donnell show up and sign on.

It's some time later in the new boys' home, and Matt comes around, looking prosperous. Father Dunne shows him around the new place, which has a school, a choir, and a swimming pool. As he's leaving, Matt drops in a donation. But it's all a front, because he's later discovered trying to burgle a local business. When the cop gives chase, Matt dodges into the boys' home and asks Father Dunne for sanctuary. Then a policeman friend of the priest arrives, and Father Dunne tells Matt to turn himself in. Instead, the boy draws a gun; and, as the police officer comes toward him, in his mind he sees the image of his father attacking, and he shoots, killing the officer.

Matt is arrested, tried, found guilty, and sentenced to hang. Father Dunne does everything he can to try and save the young man, even going to Missouri's governor, but nothing helps. So he stays with Matt until he's taken away to gallows.

Some time later, a disheartened Father Dunne is standing just outside the home he founded, seeing what's going inside through the unshuttered windows when a new small boy appears by his side and asks him if he knows how to get into Father Dunne's News Boys' Home and Protectorate. The priest tells him to just open the door and walk inside. As they step away together, we see those two footprints (from the beginning of the film) pressed into the wet cement.

Fighting Father Dunne is a touching story of love and devotion by a man who's a part of St. Louis history that is forgotten by most. But it shouldn't be. This black and white film, more than a half-century old, is a reminder that can still touch hearts decades after it was made.

Vincent Price
Born May 27, 1911

Listening to his polished and distinguished-sounding voice, most people would immediately guess that Vincent Price was a high-bred son of jolly, old England — but they would be wrong! Vincent Price was born in St. Louis and grew up on Forsyth Boulevard. His father was the owner of National Candy Company, and his grandfather was the man who invented baking powder.

A graduate of St. Louis Country Day School, Vincent Leonard Price, Jr., went to Yale University, from which he graduated in 1933, and began a teaching career in New York. But, after a year, he left to study in Britain (perhaps that's where the accent came from). A year after that, he began his acting career. After his second play, *Victoria Regina*, completed its run in London, the company decided to take the production to the U.S., and Vincent returned to his native country with a burgeoning new career. After the production's successful run on Broadway, he was offered a movie contract, but he elected to continue performing on stage instead. But he did perform on radio as a member of Orson Welles' Mercury Theatre on the Air.

Of course, Vincent did eventually opt for a film career, starting with *Service de Luxe* in 1938, followed by *The Private Lives of Elizabeth and Essex* (in which he played Sir Walter Raleigh), and another period piece set in England, *Tower of London*, both in 1939. Then, the following year, there was a film in which we barely got to see him at all but heard his distinctive voice throughout — *The Invisible Man Returns*.

In the '40s, Vincent Price's movie career really kicked into high gear, with a total of 26 films, including such productions as *The Three Musketeers; The House of the Seven Gables; The Keys of the Kingdom; The Song of Bernadette; Dragonwyck; Baghdad; Leave Her to Heaven; A Royal Scandal; Laura; The Long Night;* and *Brigham Young*.

Vincent Price (from the *Globe-Democrat* Collection at the St. Louis Mercantile Library, University of Missouri–St. Louis)

And his pace didn't slacken much in the '50s, a decade during which he appeared in 24 films. If you're keeping count, that was a total of 50 films in two decades! And that was only a portion of his theatrical work, for he did a good deal of work on radio and the new medium of television during that time period. Still, motion pictures were his primary area of concentration, and the films that Vincent Price made in the 1950s are some for which he's most often remembered. Included in this group are 1953's *House of Wax*, 1958's *The Fly*, and 1959's *Return of the Fly* and *The House on Haunted Hill*. Some of the other films he appeared in during the '50s include *The Ten Commandments*; *His Kind of Woman*; *Son of Sinbad*; *While the City Sleeps*; *The Vagabond King*; *The Bat*, *The Mad Magician*; *Adventures of Captain Fabian*; and *Casanova's Big Night*.

In the 1960s, Vincent picked up the pace even more, with 31 films, plus numerous television appearances. It was during the '60s that he began an association with American International pictures, for which he made a number of films based on stories and poems by Edgar Allan Poe: *The House of Usher*; *The Pit and the Pendulum*; *Tales of Terror*; *The Raven*; *The Haunted Palace*; *The Masque of the Red Death*; *The Tomb of Ligeia*; *The Conqueror Worm*; and *The Oblong Box*. Other '60s films include *Nefertiti*; *Master of the World*; *Twice-Told Tales*; *The Haunted Palace*; *The Comedy of Terrors*; *The Last Man on Earth*; *The Wild Weird World of Dr. Goldfoot*; and *Diary of a Madman*.

He continued to act in motion pictures throughout the '70s and '80s and into the '90s, but he made fewer major productions for theatrical release. Instead, much of his work was for television. This included hosting PBS's *Mystery!* from 1981 through 1989 and performing in several made-for-television movies. Some of his theatrical films during this period include *Cry of the Banshee*; *The Abominable Dr. Phibes*; *Theatre of Blood*; *Dr. Phibes Rises Again*; *Madhouse*; *Journey Into Fear*; *Scavenger Hunt*; *House of Long Shadows*; *The Whales of August*; *Dead Heat*; *Catchfire*; and *Edward Scissorhands*.

Also, during the last two decades of his life, Vincent concentrated more on other interests outside the realm of the dramatic arts. He authored several books, including his 1972 coffee-table edition, *A Treasury of American Art*. His appreciation for fine art was well known. In fact, he had earlier written an autobiography (in 1959), titled *I Like What I Know*, which included many remarks about his love of art. And he combined his love of fine cooking with writing and television, co-authoring several gourmet cookbooks with his second wife and co-hosting several cooking shows.

Vincent Price died in Los Angeles on October 25, 1993, at the age of 82, having appeared in more than 100 films from the 1930s through the early 1990s.

FEATURE

The Pride of St. Louis
1952

Directed by Harmon Jones

Written by Herman J. Mankiewicz and Guy Trosper

Primary Cast:

"Dizzy" Dean	Dan Dailey
Pat Dean	Joanne Dru
"Daffy" Dean	Richard Crenna
Johnny Kendall	Richard Hylton
Horst	Hugh Sanders
Moose	James Brown
Ed Monroe	Leo Cleary
Tom Weaver	Chet Huntley

What says "St. Louis" more than baseball? To many, there is nothing that expresses the spirit of ol' St. Lou better than a good slugfest at Busch Stadium. That's also why *The Pride of St. Louis* is the perfect name for a baseball movie for St. Louisans. Too bad there is very little about St. Louis in this film.

The Pride of St. Louis is the story of the great Cardinals MLB Hall of Fame pitcher Dizzy Dean. When I was growing up, Dizzy was already out of the game, but I remember his colorful commentary on radio and television. I was just a kid in the '50s, but I remember how he used to refer to himself as "Old Diz." That was about all I knew about him before I saw this movie and learned that he was one of the greatest pitchers ever to hurl a baseball.

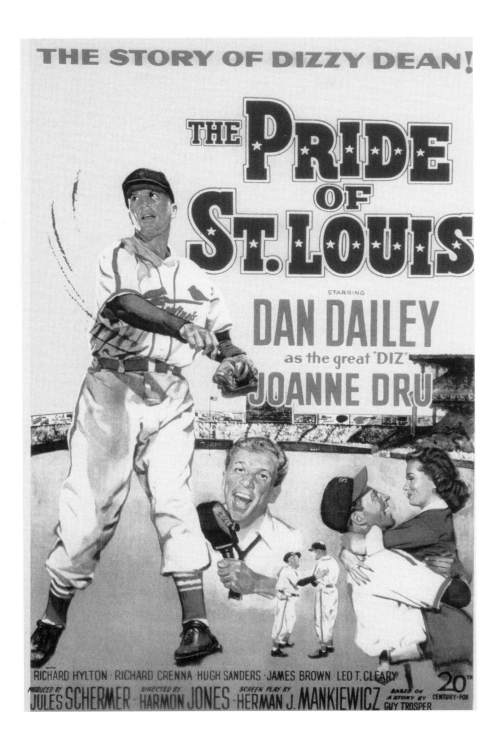

THE STORY OF DIZZY DEAN!

THE PRIDE OF ST. LOUIS

STARRING

DAN DAILEY

as the great "DIZ"

JOANNE DRU

WITH RICHARD HYLTON · RICHARD CRENNA · HUGH SANDERS · JAMES BROWN · LEO T. CLEARY

PRODUCED BY JULES SCHERMER · DIRECTED BY HARMON JONES · SCREEN PLAY BY HERMAN J. MANKIEWICZ · BASED ON A STORY BY GUY TROSPER

20TH CENTURY-FOX

His real name was Jay Hanna Dean, but you don't learn that in this film. Apparently, "Ol' Diz" didn't care much for his real name, so he told people that he was Jerome Herman Dean, and that's the name that you'll hear throughout in *The Pride of St. Louis* – that and, of course, "Dizzy Dean."

Watching this film, you get the idea that Dizzy Dean was a braggart, and he was. "Anybody who's ever had the privilege of seein' me play ball knows that I am the greatest pitcher in the world. And them that ain't been fortunate enough to have a gander at Ol' Diz in action can look at the records," Diz is reported to have said. He didn't mind telling folks about his abilities, but he could definitely back up his claims.

This production opens with a young Dean pitching barefoot in his native Ozarks. The role of Diz is played throughout the film by Dan Dailey, who appears too old to play the part, but he certainly has mastered Dean's folksy mannerisms and language. When a Cardinals scout who has been watching the barefoot pitcher in action tells Dean that he wants the young ballplayer to report to the team's farm club in Houston, Diz contends that it's a waste of good talent for him to pitch for a minor league club and that he should just go directly to the Cardinals. He also encourages the scout to go ahead and sign up his brother Paul (played by Richard Crenna), who is also a pitcher. The scout declines Diz's request on both counts, so the young, uneducated, hillbilly pitcher reports to Houston to begin his professional career.

In his new surroundings, Diz doesn't waste any time in letting others know that he thinks he's the best pitcher Houston has and that he should be sent on to the big-league St. Louis Cardinals. One of those he tries to impress is a young female credit manager, Pat Nash (Joanne Dru), at a department store, where he's pick out a new suit to replace his old backwoods garments and charged the outfit to the Houston ball club. When he insists that she meet him for "supper," she politely refuses, but young Diz will have none of that, instead telling her when he'll pick her up. As he's walking away, she asks the brash young Dean if he doesn't need her address, which she proceeds to give him.

When Diz's brother, Paul (later known as "Daffy" Dean), comes down to Houston to see his brother pitch, Diz takes him to where Pat is sitting in the stadium with another man and introduces the two, then asks the couple if Paul can sit in their box so he won't be lonely. Diz later tells his brother that he's "crazy about" Pat, and he soon proceeds to take Pat off the dating market by putting a ladder to her bedroom window in the middle of the night, climbing up, and asking her to marry him. The only option he'll give her is when: that night, the next morning, or the next afternoon. She chooses the latter.

We see Diz pitching in a lot of games, blowing away Houston's competition, along with the obligatory newspaper headlines proclaiming how well Diz is pitching. Sure enough, he soon joins the Cardinals and proves just as effective in the Big League. When he's joined by his brother on the Cardinals roster, the duo prove to be just too much for the Cardinals' opponents. On one occasion, Diz pitched the first game of a double header, which the Cardinals won in a shutout. Daffy pitched the second game and had a no-hitter. Afterward (in front of the media), Diz told his brother: "If'n you'd only tole me you was gonna pitch a no-hitter, I'da pitched me one, too."

At the beginning of the 1934 season, Diz declared that he would win 30 games that year and that Daffy would win 15. As it turned out, he did win exactly 30 games, and his brother exceeded Diz's boast by winning 19. Before the World Series that year, Diz went on record again: "Who won the Pennant?" he asked in a statement to the press, then answered his own question: "Me and Paul. Who's going to win the Series? Me and Paul." And they did. Against the Detroit Tigers, each pitched two games and won all four, thereby winning the World Series for the Cardinals, as Diz had predicted.

In the years of 1932 through 1936, Dizzy Dean won 120 games for the Cardinals. In four of those five seasons, he led the National League in strikeouts and in complete games pitched.

After Daffy was injured in a fluke "come-backer" hit off his hand, he retired from baseball. Then, in 1937, Dizzy developed a soreness in his pitching arm. He lost much of his effectiveness on the mound, and was traded to the Chicago Clubs the following year. This film shows how Diz struggled to return to his glory days as a pitcher, but it never happened. Eventually, he was sent back down to the minor league, where he played for Tulsa and was so ineffective that he was released.

After this major tragedy in his life, Dizzy went into denial and even tried (unsuccessfully) to get other Major League teams to pick him up. In this film, we see him refusing to accept that his career in the game that he loved was over. A distressed Pat urges her husband to try something else, maybe taking a job in sales, but he'll have nothing of it, taking up drinking (Diz had always been a teetotaler) and gambling. Finally, after Pat has had enough and leaves him, Diz finally realizes that he must move on with his life. That's when his other career as a baseball commentator begins, but it isn't without controversy.

Dizzy Dean may have been "the pride of St. Louis," but he didn't instill the same pride among educators, many of whom were up in arms because of his jargon, declaring to his employers that his language was a detriment to Diz's young listeners. But Diz's boss refuses to fire the baseball great, instead deferring to Diz's way of talking. That's when Diz announces on the air that he is giving up his career as a commentator, to the astonishment of his fellow announcer, Tom Weaver (played by NBC News great Chet Huntley).

But Diz's fans won't let it end that way for their hero. An outpouring of support leads to the educators withdrawing their opposition to his on-air presence. And, of course, Pat comes home to her happy husband.

In the latter half of the 20th century, many have become acquainted with native St. Louisan Yogi Berri and his outlandish pronouncements, which have come to be known as "Yogisms." But Yogi was definitely preceded by another colorful ballplayer, who called himself Dizzy Dean. Unfortunately, the makers of this film chose to leave out some of the more outstanding "Dizzyisms" (including several I've mentioned in this chapter). Perhaps this was an attempt to show respect for Diz, but by leaving these remarks out of the film, the filmmakers have in fact detracted from one of the most beloved "characters" baseball has ever known.

The Pride of St. Louis came out in 1952 and is definitely a period piece. "They don't make 'em like this any more." But it can be an enjoyable film to watch both for baseball fans, in general, and Cardinals fans, in particular. For those who see this film hoping to catch some glimpse of St. Louis of bygone days, forget it! The film doesn't so much as mention a street address. But it is the story of one of the greatest pitchers to play for St. Louis' beloved Cardinals, so it certainly must be considered in any selection of films about the Cardinals' home town.

STAR

Betty Grable
Born December 18, 1916

Betty Grable was called "the girl with the million-dollar legs" and was the fantasy woman for many a GI during World War II. Her swimsuit photo, showing the movie star looking backward over her right shoulder, is one of the most famous shots ever taken. Betty's film career started in 1929 and lasted just over two-and-a-half decades. Still, during that time period, she appeared in 80 productions.

Elizabeth Ruth Grable was born in St. Louis in 1916. Her mother was determined to see her daughter become a star, so she enrolled little Betty in Clark's Dancing School at the age of three. By the time Betty was 13 years old, her mother had already moved with her daughter to Hollywood, determined to see Betty in film. It must have worked because Betty appeared in her first film, *Happy Days*, before she was 14.

Her mother was so determined that young Betty have a career in film that she obtained forged papers allowing her daughter to dance in the chorus line of the 1930 film *Let's Go Places* when she was yet 13, even though the law required chorus dances to be over 15.

By the time Betty was 16, she had already appeared in 18 productions, including *New Movietone Follies of 1930; Crashing Hollywood; Ex-Sweeties; Lady Please; Hollywood Luck; Probation; The Flirty Sleepwalker; Hollywood Lights; The Age of Consent; Hold 'Em Jail;* and *The Kid from Spain.*

In 1933-34, Betty made another 15 films (for a total of 33 films between her 13th and 18th birthdays). Some of the productions from these two years are *Calvalcade; Child of Manhattan; Melody Cruise; Sweetheart of Sigma Chi; School for Romance; Love Detectives; Elmer Steps Out; Business Is a Pleasure; Susie's Affairs; The Gay Divorcee; Student Tour;* and *By Your Leave.*

During the rest of the 1930s, she made 18 films, at a somewhat slower pace, perhaps because she was taking on bigger and better roles. Some of

Betty Grable (from the *Globe-Democrat* Collection at the St. Louis Mercantile Library, University of Missouri–St. Louis)

these are *The Nitwits*; *A Night at the Biltmore Bowl*; *Drawing Rumors*; *Old Man Rhythm*; *Collegiate*; *Follow the Fleet*; *Pigskin Parade*; *This Way Please*; *Thrill of a Lifetime*; *College Swing*; *Give Me a Sailor*; *Campus Confessions*; *Man About Town*; *The Day the Bookies Wept*; and the film that defined her for the rest of her life, *Million Dollar Legs*.

Betty appeared in 21 films in the whole of the 1940s, including *Down Argentine Way*; *Tin Pan Alley*; *Moon Over Miami*; *I Wake Up Screaming*; *Song of the Islands*; *Footlight Serenade*; *Springtime in the Rockies*; *Coney Island*; *Sweet Rosie O'Grady*; *Pin Up Girl*; *The Dolly Sisters*; *Hollywood Park*; *The Shocking Miss Pilgrim*; *Mother Wore Tights*; *That Lady in Ermine*; *When My Baby Smiles at Me*; and *The Beautiful Blonde from Bashful Bend*.

Betty ended her film career in 1955, the year she turned 39 years old. Some of her last productions are *Wabash Avenue*, *My Blue Heaven*, *Meet Me After the Show*, *The Farmer Takes a Wife*, *How to Marry a Millionaire*, and *Three for the Show*. Her last movie was *How to Be Very, Very Popular*.

During World War II, Betty spent a lot of time touring, entertaining American troops, and showing off her famous legs, which Twentieth Century Fox had insured for $1,250,000.

Betty Grable was married to former child star Jackie Coogan from 1937 to 1940, then to band leader Harry James from 1943 to 1965. She died of lung cancer on July 2, 1973, in Santa Monica, California, at the age of 56.

Betty Grable (from the *Globe-Democrat* Collection at the St. Louis Mercantile Library, University of Missouri–St. Louis)

The Spirit of St. Louis
1957

Directed by Billy Wilder

Written by Charles A. Lindbergh (book); Charles Lederer, Wendell Mayes, and Billy Wilder (screenplay)

Primary Cast:

Charles A. Lindbergh	James Stewart
Bud Gurney	Murray Hamilton
Frank Mahoney	Bartlett Robinson
Father Hussman	Marc Connelly
Donald Hall	Arthur Space
O.W. Schultz	Charles Watts
Harold Bixby	David Orrick McDearmon
E. Lansing Ray	Maurice Manson
Major Albert Lambert	Robert Burton
Charles Levine	Richard Deacon
Harry Knight	Robert Cornthwaite
Girl with mirror	Patricia Smith
Captain at Brooks Field	Carleton Young
Jess, the cook	Johnny Lee
Secretary	Virginia Christine
Surplus dealer	Olin Howland
San Diego reporter	Robert Williams

Even though you know perfectly well what's going to happen in *The Spirit of St. Louis* — that "Lucky Lindy" is going to fly across the Atlantic from New York to Paris — taking that flight with Jimmy Stewart fills you with excitement and suspense from the moment the plane takes off until it lands more than 3,000 miles and 33 hours later.

Though very little of this story actually takes place in St. Louis, the true events that inspired this film occurred because of the financial backing of several well-off St. Louisans, who believed in the young mail pilot and his plan to fly solo across that great body of water and, thereby, accomplish something that had never before been done in the history of the world!

The story opens in New York's Garden City Hotel, where a large group of reporters have set themselves up in the lobby, waiting for Charles Lindbergh (James Stewart) to make his move. Inside his hotel room, a restless young "Slim" (as practically everyone in the film calls young Lindbergh) is trying to get some sleep. His friend, Frank Mahoney (Bartlett Robinson), is sitting outside his room to keep curious reporters away from the youthful pilot.

Inside, Slim is having no luck sleeping. It's raining outside, and he's worried that he won't be able to take off for Paris the next morning, as he had wanted. He's also too nervous, and he starts thinking back (in flashback form) on the events that brought him to his present situation.

In the first flashback, we see an even younger Lindbergh as an airmail pilot who flies letters from St. Louis to Chicago and around other Midwest locales. We also see that the young pilot is practically fearless. After refueling, he takes off in fog so thick he can hardly see in front of his own face. When his plane starts to go down, he calmly stands up in his seat, with his mail in hand, and jumps out of the plane, his parachute unfolding above him. Since "the mail must get through," he boards a train with his mail still in tow. On the train, speaking with a suspenders salesman (Charles Watts), we get to know something about the character and dedication of the man who would soon make the first successful solo, nonstop airplane flight across the ocean.

Next, Lindbergh comes into a St. Louis diner, where he makes a three-minute long-distance call for $5 (quite a sum of money back in the 1920s) to a New York aircraft manufacturer. He states that he's representing a group of prominent St. Louis businessmen interested in buying one of their planes to fly to Paris. Afterward, he observes, "Now all I have to do is find a group of prominent businessmen with $15,000."

After six weeks of talking and negotiating, Slim still has no takers on his proposal. That's when he calls on Harold Bixby (David Orrick McDearmon), president of the St. Louis Chamber of Commerce, E. Lansing Ray (Maurice Manson), editor of the *St. Louis Globe-Democrat*, and Major Albert Lambert (Robert Burton), for whom St. Louis Lambert International Airport would one day be named, as well as other business leaders. When he explains his idea about crossing the Atlantic in a single-engine craft, the men have several pertinent questions — but Bixby even comes up with the famous name for Lindbergh's aircraft that now is known the world over (should the group decide to sponsor Lindbergh, that is).

Then we see young Lindbergh all dressed up, calling on the president of the Columbia Aircraft Company in New York City. Slim has a check in hand from his St. Louis backers to pay for the plane, but when the official (Richard Deacon) tells Lindbergh that he will sell the plane only if Columbia gets to pick the pilot for the New York to Paris flight, Slim walks out on the deal.

As soon as he arrives back in St. Louis, Lindbergh is sent out again, this time to California to meet with some other aircraft builders. He finds these men a great deal less formal. This group is working out of a very modest factory, is led by Frank Mahoney and calls itself the Ryan Airlines Company. They are ready and eager to build the plane to Lindbergh's specifications.

There are several interesting scenes showing the design and construction of what came to be known as "The Spirit of St. Louis." After the craft is completed significantly ahead of schedule, Lindbergh takes it out on its test spins above San Diego. Just as the group is about to take a "graduation" photo, Slim gets news that two very experienced French pilots have taken off from Paris to New York. Now, Lindbergh is uncertain what he should do, but he flies the new plane back to St. Louis anyway. There, he discovers that the two French fliers and their plane are missing. His backers give Slim a chance to pull out on his commitment, but he isn't interested. So it's on to New York for the young pilot.

Intermittent with the flashback scenes we see Lindbergh lying in his bed at the Garden City Hotel, remembering the events that brought him there and trying to go to sleep, all to no avail.

Finally, morning arrives, and he heads out to the Roosevelt Field, along with an entourage of followers. The rain is still coming down slowly, but after checking out the muddy airstrip, he decides to proceed with his plan. It takes a number of men to help push him off on the soggy ground, but finally Lindbergh is rolling down the waterlogged field. He takes off beyond the point where he should and barely clears the electrical wires and the trees.

Soon, Slim discovers that he has an unexpected stowaway, a common housefly, to which he talks often as he flies out of the rain over Boston and Canada. Finally, just as he is about to leave the last bit of land behind, the fly leaves him all to himself. But he keeps on talking just the same.

As he flies over that lonely body of water, already exhausted from lack of sleep, Lindbergh knows that he has perhaps 40 more hours that he must stay awake to get to Paris, and he recalls some more of the events that propelled him to attempt to do what no one else had ever done before.

We see Slim buying his first airplane: how he rode his Harley-Davidson motorcycle down to Georgia to find a surplus airplane dealer (Olin Howland) and purchased a rickety old World War II leftover, trading in the motorcycle as part of the deal. When he's readying himself to take off in this worn-out looking monstrosity, he reveals to the other man that he's never flown solo before. But there doesn't seem to be much fear in Charles Lindbergh. After lots of bumps and starts and ups and downs, he at last is off in his first very own airplane.

Between the flashbacks, there is plenty of tension, first with the rain-drenched airfield, then with the danger of flying into trees or wires because of his tardy liftoff. Next, as he's nearing the end of the Canadian land mass, Slim runs into a patch of fog that he has to fly under. Over the ocean, he loses his bearings, uncertain how far off course he has drifted. On one occasion, his wings become encased in ice, and he must find warmer air to melt away the frozen liquid before his plane conks out. Then, throughout the flight, there is a real and present danger that he will fall asleep and crash, unnoticed, into the gaping Atlantic Ocean. Lindbergh does, in fact, nod off from time to time, but each time he awakens in time to avoid a collision with the waters.

Among the other flashbacks taken from his memory are those of his days as an even younger pilot (Lindbergh was only 25 when he made his famous flight across the ocean). In one of these, we see Lindbergh as a hawker, offering to take any and all takers up for a spin in the clouds for the measly sum of $5.

Then there's his encounter with fellow "sky gypsy" Bud Gurney (Murray Hamilton) as both men are in flight in separate planes. They signal to each other and eventually set their planes down in a farmer's field, then sit around talking about their flying experiences. After that, they decide to "hook up" and perform stunts at air shows throughout the Midwest.

And we see his landing at the Brooks Field Flight School, uninvited, and how much it disturbs the instructor (Carleton Young) that a bold young pilot would have the audacity to land such a beaten-up plane on his airstrip and then expect to attend the academy.

After the last of these flashback ends, we see Lindbergh peering out the side of his plane, spying a seagull, and deducing that he must be approaching land. He circles a small fishing vessel below, shouting to its lone passenger, but the man doesn't respond, so Lindbergh flies on. Eventually, he comes to an outcropping of huge boulders protruding from the ocean, and, shortly thereafter, he comes, at long last, upon land. Finally, he realizes that he is where he wants to be — flying over Ireland. He shouts down at the people below, and they look up and eagerly wave to the young man in his flying machine.

As he flies onward and over England, Lindbergh realizes that's it's a simple matter to skip over the English Channel, then just follow the Seine River down to his destination, Paris. And that is just what he does. When he reaches Paris, Lindbergh has to search through the mass of city lights, somewhat disorientedly, until he finds LeBourget Field, and there he gently sets the "Spirit of St. Louis" on land once more. When he does, almost at once, he is mobbed by the gigantic crowd that has gathered awaiting his arrival — a group comprised of more than 200,000 people, Jimmy Stewart reveals in his voice-over narration. Then, in the film's final scene, we see what appears to be the actual ticker-tape parade of Lindbergh down the streets of New York City. This time, Stewart's voice reveals that there were 4 million people who greeted him upon his triumphant return.

The Spirit of St. Louis is still an exciting and engaging motion picture almost a half-century after it was made. The use of flashbacks makes the story move along much more briskly than it would had we simply been trapped inside the cockpit with Jimmy Stewart throughout the more than two hours of this film.

The choice of Stewart to play "Lucky Lindy" is, at once, both an appealing and a quizzical one. Charles A. Lindbergh was only 25 when he made his famous flight across the Atlantic, yet Jimmy Stewart was almost twice that age when he made this film (he was 49 when the production was released). It's obvious that Stewart isn't the young man he's portraying; nevertheless, he offers a very compelling performance that should satisfy most students of modern history.

And though St. Louis appears very little in this production, it *is* a true and delightful tale of the *spirit* of a few Gateway City entrepreneurs, who were willing to back a bold and risky plan that put their city's name out front for all the world to see.

Phyllis Diller
Born July 17, 1917

She had wanted to become a concert pianist, but Phyllis Diller became known as one of this country's zaniest female comics instead.

Born in Ohio, she moved to Webster Groves in 1961. Appearing at St. Louis area nightclubs, she polished the standup routine that eventually took her to national prominence.

Phyllis made her first screen appearance in *Splendor in the Grass* the same year that she relocated to St. Louis. But it was 1966 that was her "breakout" year. By then, the country had discovered her wild talent, so that year she co-starred with Bob Hope in *Boy, Did I Get a Wrong Number!* and starred in *The Fat Spy*. That same year, she also became the star of her own network TV show, *The Pruitts of Southampton*; however, the program wasn't a big success and was cancelled after 30 episodes. In re-runs, the show is often known as *The Phyllis Diller Show*.

She did another six movies in the remaining three years of the '60s: *Mad Monster Party* (in which she was the voice of the Monster's Mate); *Eight on the Lam*; *Silent Treatment*; *The Private Navy of Sgt. O'Farrell*; *The Adding Machine*; and *Did You Hear the One About the Traveling Saleslady?*

In the 1970s and '80s, Phyllis did very few films, instead concentrating on her standup act. She again lent the use of her distinctive voice to two productions: *The Mad, Mad, Mad Comedians* and *Alice Through the Looking Glass*. She appeared in *A Pleasure Doing Business*, *Pink Motel*, and *Doctor Hackenstein*.

In the 1990s, she appeared in *Pucker Up and Bark Like a Dog*, *The Boneyard*, *The Perfect Man*, *The Silence of the Hams*, and *The Debtors*. Her voice was featured in *The Nutcracker Prince*, *Happily Ever After*, *A Bug's Life*, *The Nuttiest Nutcracker*, and in the animated TV series *Captain Planet and the Planeteers*.

She has already appeared in seven films since the year 2000: *Everything's*

Phyllis Diller (from the *Globe-Democrat* Collection at the St. Louis Mercantile Library, University of Missouri–St. Louis)

Jake; The Last Place on Earth; Motocross Kids; West From North Goes South; Unbeatable Harold; Forget About It; and *Hip! Edgy! Quirky!*

Actually, Phyllis Diller was first seen nationally in 1950 as a contestant on Groucho Marx's *You Bet Your Life* television program — long before she became known for her nightclub act in which she berated her fictitious husband, "Fang."

And although she is remembered far and wide for her outrageous comedy, Phyllis never gave up on her early goal of being a concert pianist. The fact is that she has appeared across the country as a solo pianist with more than 100 of the nation's leading symphony orchestras.

The Great St. Louis Bank Robbery
1959

Directed by Charles Guggenheim and John Stix
Written by Richard T. Heffron

Primary Cast:

George Fowler	*Steve McQueen*
John Egan	*Crahan Denton*
Gino	*David Clarke*
Willie	*James Dukas*
Ann	*Molly McCarthy*
Eddie	*Larry Gerst*
Eddie's Wife	*Martha Gable*
Ann's Boyfriend	*Frank Novotny*
Bank Officer	*Boyd Williams*
Phone Repairman	*Robert Klauss*
St. Louis Police	*Themselves*

If you've lived in St. Louis a long time, you may well recognize many of the locales as they existed in the 1950s (before the Arch towered over the riverfront) in the true crime drama, *The Great St. Louis Bank Robbery*.

Starring a youthful Steve McQueen when his career was just beginning (but after he quit calling himself "Steven McQueen," as he did in *The Blob* the previous year), this 1959 black and white film tells the story of the attempted robbery of St. Louis' Southwest Bank, located at Southwest Avenue and Kingshighway Boulevard.

Note the misspelling of Steve McQueen's name on this French movie poster for *The Great St. Louis Bank Robbery*

The film starts with three cars pulling into Tower Grove Park, and four men getting out and walking to one of the picnic pavilions. Three of the men are dressed pretty much as 1950s businessmen, except without the ties, but with the hats. One is dressed differently. He looks considerably younger, is wearing a college letterman jacket, and has no hat. This is George Fowler (Steve McQueen).

John Egan (Crahan Denton), the oldest of the four and obviously the man in charge, introduces himself to Fowler, who stands a little distance away from the other three and seems to feel out of place. Right away, Willie (James Dukas) starts challenging George and poking fun at him for the way he's dressed, but Gino (David Clarke), who came in the car with George, comes to the younger man's defense.

It seems that Gino has brought in young George as the getaway driver for the group, but Steve McQueen's character has no experience in driving during a robbery, and he hasn't even spent any time in "the joint." These facts make Willie and Egan somewhat nervous about working with the young man. "I don't like going out with somebody I don't know," Egan declares. But Gino retorts: "I know him. I know him since he's a kid. He can drive okay, and he's got the nerve."

Soon, Egan focuses the men on why they've come together — on the task at hand, planning the robbery of the Southwest Bank. He pulls a paper out of his attaché case, declaring: "This looks like a good one. Never been touched. No bank guard. Good location." Egan goes on to briefly discuss the upcoming "bank job" and how long he thinks it will take to "case" the financial institution in question. He hands the other members of the group schedule cards for them to use in their observation of the bank.

Egan also stresses to the other three men: "One thing more: No women! If you have the brains you were born with, you ought to know it."

When Gino asks Egan if he will "bankroll" the group, Egan says he has the money to cover himself and Willie, but the other two will have to provide their own lodging and "eating" money. But this causes a problem that will ultimately be the group's undoing. While Egan is still talking to Willie, Gino and George start to walk way, and Gino tells George that he'll have to contact Ann (Molly McCarthy) to see about getting $50 to carry them through until the robbery. George resists: "I don't want to see her." But Gino tells him to just go see her and tell her the money's for him. After all, he is her brother, and he "never blamed" George for what happened, but now the younger man has to go see Ann and get some money for them to live on.

As a sort of test for George, Egan rides with the young man to a parking lot where he tells him he has to steal a license plate off a car. At first, George insists that he only agreed to drive the getaway vehicle and that he's no "petty thief." Eventually, however, he relents; he nervously locates a target plate and starts to remove it when the car drives away. He's a little unnerved, but he notices a woman just driving up, and he decides to take the plate off the back of her car when she's parked.

Afterward, from a phone booth, George calls Ann at work, and, reluctantly, she agrees to meet him at a bar that evening. When they do get together, she seems very cool to him, but he eventually asks for the $50, declaring that the money's for her brother. She takes out her checkbook and starts to write a check, saying if the money is really for Gino, there shouldn't be any problem with her making the check out to Gino, obviously suspicious that the money isn't for her brother, at all. But George tells her that making the check out to her brother is just fine.

Egan and Willie are sharing a room at a cheap hotel, but Willie complains about sharing the bathroom and complains more about using George on the job. Meanwhile, Egan sits at the desk, still planning the robbery in detail. The next day, Egan marches into the bank like a normal customer, even stopping at the entrance to make a contribution to someone collecting for charity. Inside, he observes the bank's arrangement and where all the officials are sitting, making notes and diagrams. Before he leaves the facility, he stops by one of the tellers and gets change, making some brief conversation, as any customer might.

The men take turns watching the bank from across the street in a diner. George comes in, and Gino leaves. But just at that moment, Ann is coming out of the bank, and she spots her brother get in a car and drive away. She goes inside the diner and sees George. When she walks up to him, she announces that she knows what's going on. At first, George insists nothing is going on, but she starts to get loud, so he asks her to please meet him later so they can talk.

Later, as the four men are discussing their plans at Tower Grove Park, Willie accuses George of messing around with a girl, saying he saw them together in the diner. George insists there's nothing to what Willie is claiming.

Again, Egan has to referee: "I don't care whether you like each other or not. You keep your personal feelings out of this."

Egan insists they make a dry run, with George driving the four, as he is supposed to do during the actual robbery. They drive the planned course, stopping and timing each step of their actions.

That night, Ann again meets with George, and he tries to convince her he's a salesman in St. Louis to peddle his wares. But she isn't buying any of it. She quizzes him on what he's selling and how much it costs. She continues to press him, indicating again that she knows what's going on. George relents somewhat, insisting: "I'm driving a car. That's all." But Ann tells him to get out while he still can — before he ruins his life.

"If you do this thing," she declares, "you'll run yourself rotten. Another Gino. Pretty soon, you won't remember you were anything else. I don't know if I can let you do this."

Contemplating Ann's comments later in a bar with John Egan, he asks the other man if he's ever known anyone who pulled just one job and got out. Egan tries to tell him there have been such men, but he doesn't sound convincing. Then, when a woman approaches their table, Egan chases her away, telling her to "get away, tramp." He later tells George that his mother was a drunk who made him buy booze for her before she fell down the stairs in a drunken stupor and died.

Meanwhile, Ann is out on a date with Pat (Frank Novotny). After they leave the bar where they've been, she seems somewhat drunk and insists on walking by Southwest Bank to see if her money is okay. Later, while he has his back toward her, she takes out lipstick and writes, "Warning: You will be robbed." When he sees what she's done, Pat is very upset and storms off.

In the middle of the night, Egan and Willie storm in on George and Gino, who were asleep. They tell the other two men about the writing on the bank window. After interrogating George, who admits talking to Ann, the three men go to her apartment. Ann is frightened, but Gino tells his sister it will be all right, but she has to get out of St. Louis for a few days. Egan makes George leave; George tells Gino to keep an eye on the two other men with his sister. Eventually, Gino is sent away, too, and Egan is escorting Ann down the fire escape with her suitcase. When they get into a verbal confrontation, a scuffle follows, and Ann falls to her death.

Steve McQueen in the lobby of Southwest Bank (Courtesy of Ivy Classics, Inc.)

(Courtesy of Ivy Classics, Inc)

GSL-4

The time has come for the actual bank robbery, but Egan has decided to make some changes. Instead of George, Willie will be the driver. Now, George will have to work inside the bank holding off hostages while Gino collects the money in the cash drawers.

Things go pretty much as planned during the robbery. Egan has allowed two minutes to collect the money and leave, but that isn't enough time. After an alarm buzzer is tripped by a teller, the police arrive much more quickly than the gang's boss has anticipated. With the police now on the scene, Willie starts the getaway car and abandons the others. In a shootout, Egan tries to escape, holding a female bank customer as a hostage in front of him, but he's gunned down.

Now, Gino, who's already awaiting trial on another charge, starts shouting that he's never going back (to prison), and he runs downstairs in the bank trying to find a way out. When he finds none, he shoots himself.

So that leaves only George, who has been wounded in the leg, and he also tries to take a female hostage, but her husband confronts him. He drops his gun, insisting he's not like the other men, that he's really not a bad person. Then the police storm the bank; they drag the frightened George to the waiting paddy wagon and drive away. And that's how the story ends, without a closing, wrap-up scene as we've come to expect in modern films.

Certainly, *The Great St. Louis Bank Robbery* does have some large "holes" in its storyline. For instance, we learn that George and Ann were in college somewhere but were expelled together for some unexplained reason. We know that Gino's awaiting trial for another crime, but we're never told what. Perhaps these and other explanations were in the original story but were edited out. But probably not. Standards have changed over the years. Decades ago, movies were shorter and choppier than today primarily because they didn't have to fill a full, two-hour time slot. In the '30s, '40s, and '50s, the "feature" was only part of the bill. There usually were cartoons, "shorts," and often newsreels shown along with the main film, so movies were usually less than an hour-and-a-half in length (this one is 1:25).

Even though *The Great St. Louis Bank Robbery* isn't a major "classic" movie, it does offer some decent character development. We get to know the four robbers fairly well, along with Ann, George's former girlfriend. In this film, we meet a young Steve McQueen, who's still getting to know the craft of acting; however, he does make us feel for him, as does Molly McCarthy as

Ann. Also, we come to realize that Egan has a serious problem with women, which foreshadows the confrontation that leads to Ann's death. The character of the other two, although touched on, is developed less fully.

Still and all, it's interesting to see those black and white scenes of St. Louis as it appeared in the 1950s in what is generally an acceptable period film.

Actor Frank Novotny is shown here outside of Southwest Bank
(Courtesy of Ivy Classics, Inc.)

Shelley Winters
Born August 18, 1920

She was born Shirley Schrift and lived her early years on St. Louis' Newstead Avenue, but the world came to know her as Oscar winner Shelley Winters.

Her mother had been an opera singer and her father worked in a tailor shop as young Shirley was growing up. Before she began school, she was already showing signs of the talent that would lead to her lifelong career in acting: At age four, she took part in the Veiled Prophet pageant. After her father moved his family to New York City so he could work in the garment district there, she began studying at the Actors Studio.

She did some modeling and was a chorus girl, and then, at age 20, she was cast on Broadway in *The Night Before Christmas*; three years later, she signed on with Columbia Pictures. In her first three films, she had uncredited bit parts; then, in 1944, she received her first credited role as "young woman" in *Together Again*. That same year, she appeared in *Knickerbocker Holiday, She's a Soldier, Nine Girls, Sailor's Holiday,* and *Cover Girl*.

Largely considered her first outstanding movie performance was her role as Pat Kroll in 1947's *Double Life*, where she played a waitress who falls for a Shakespearean actor (Ronald Colman). This production also featured her first film death scene, something she subsequently repeated in a number of other movies.

Also in 1947, Shelley returned to Broadway to play Ado Annie in the musical *Oklahoma!*

During the late '40s, she appeared in a number of films, including *A Thousand and One Nights; Tonight and Every Night; Cry of the City; Take One False Step; Larceny; Red River;* and *The Great Gatsby*. Then, in 1951, for her portrayal of meek factory worker Alice Tripp in *A Place in the Sun*, she was nominated for her first Oscar.

Shelley Winters (from the *Globe-Democrat* Collection at the St. Louis Mercantile Library, University of Missouri–St. Louis)

Some of Shelley's other '50s films include *The Raging Tide; He Ran All the Way; Untamed Frontier; Phone Call From a Stranger; Tennessee Champ; Playgirl; Executive Suite; I Died a Thousand Times;* and *The Night of the Hunter.*

In the 1960s, Shelley performed in such productions as *Lolita; The Chapman Report; Wives and Lovers; The Three Sisters; Alfie; Enter Laughing; Harper; Wild in the Streets; A House Is Not a Home;* and *The Greatest Story Ever Told.*

Among her films in the '70s were *Bloody Mama; Pete's Dragon; City on Fire; Cleopatra Jones; Journey Into Fear; Something to Hide; Black Journal, That Lucky Touch; A Very Little Man; The Tenant;* and *What's the Matter with Helen?*

Shelley's movie career continued through the 1980s and '90s with such productions as *Fanny Hill; The Delta Force; Over the Brooklyn Bridge; Very Close Quarters; Purple People Eater; Touch of a Stranger; Raging Angels; Stepping Out; Jury Duty; Portrait of a Lady; Gideon;* and *La Bomba.*

All told, since her motion picture career began in 1943, Shelley Winters appeared in more than 100 films. Throughout her career, she was often recognized for her acting ability. She received Oscars for both 1959's *The Diary of Anne Frank* and 1965's *A Patch of Blue.* She received a Golden Globe Award for her performance in 1972's *The Poseidon Adventure.* Also, she won an Emmy for television's *Two is the Number* in 1964 and a Venice Film Festival Prize for *Executive Suite* in 1954.

Shelley Winters died of heart failure on January 14, 2006, in Beverly Hills, California. She was 85.

The Hoodlum Priest
1961

Directed by Irvin Kershner
Written by Joseph Landon and Don Murray

Primary Cast:

Father Charles Dismas Clark	*Don Murray*
Billy Lee Jackson	*Keir Dullea*
Ellen Henley	*Cindi Wood*
Louis Rosen	*Larry Gates*
George McHale	*Logan Ramsey*
Pio Gentile	*Don Joslyn*
Mario Mazziotti	*Sam Capuano*
Angelo Mazzioti	*Lou Martini*
Assistant District Attorney	*Vince O'Brien*
Judge Garrity	*Al Mack*
Father Dunne	*Norman McKay*
Hector Sterne	*Joseph Cusanelli*
Weasel	*Bill Atwood*
Detective Shattuck	*Roger Ray*
Governor	*Ralph Peterson*
Prisoner	*Jack Eigen*
Father David Michaels	*Walter L. Wiedmer*
Genny	*Kelly Stephens*

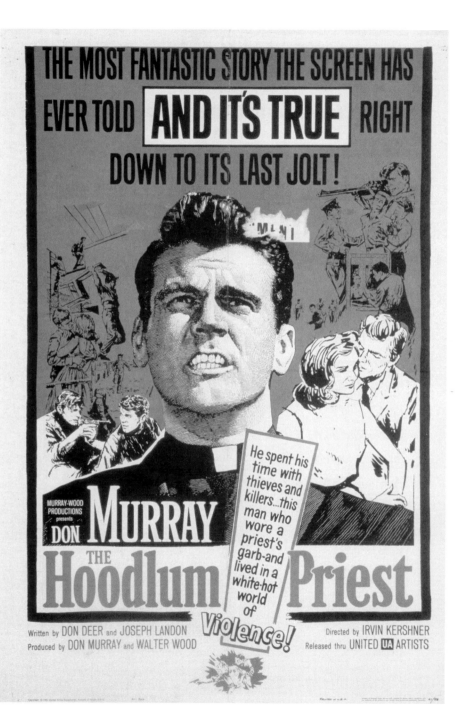

| Warden | Warren Parker |
| Prison Chaplin | Joseph Hamilton |

The title of this film suggests that this is the story of a corrupt clergyman, but it's just the opposite. *The Hoodlum Priest* is the true story of a St. Louis chaplain who was dedicated to helping ex-convicts return to society and lead productive, non-criminal lives.

The brainchild of actor Don Murray, who co-wrote the screenplay (using the name Don Deer), produced this motion picture, and starred in the title role, *The Hoodlum Priest* was filmed as well as set in St. Louis. It shares a storyline with an earlier production, *Fighting Father Dunne*, as both are true tales of St. Louis priests fighting to establish homes for the outcasts of society, and both movies come to the same disturbing conclusion. (And there's even a Father Dunne in this film, although, since the events occur more than a half-century apart, it's unlikely that this is same Father Dunne that Pat O'Brien played in the earlier production.)

This story opens with a prisoner being released from the penitentiary in Jefferson City and escorted to a train by a prison guard. The convict, Billy Lee Jackson, is played by Keir Dullea in his first theatrical motion picture, a few years before Stanley Kubrick cast him in the lead role (as Dave Bowman) in the now-classic *2001: A Space Odyssey*.

Moments after Billy is on the train bound for St. Louis, he's met by his buddy, Pio Gentile (Don Joslyn). The two hang out together in St. Louis for a while, doing such things as checking out the local burlesque houses. Then Pio takes Billy to meet another man, where they discuss a robbery. However, the other is suspicious of Billy's credentials, quizzing him about why he spent two years in the pen. Keir Dullea's character finally confesses that it was for an armed robbery in which he netted only $19. Eventually, Billy bolts and runs out of the man's apartment. That's when the other man, Father Charles Clark (Don Murray), walks across the room and puts on his clerical collar, and Pio accuses him of scaring Billy off.

Next, Father Clark is off to the jail, where he's admitted without question. Inside, he talks with several of those incarcerated about their cases, even offering to find a good attorney to defend one who strongly protests his innocence.

From the St. Louis City Jail, it's short bus ride for Father Clark across town to the Jesuit high school where he teaches. There, he's met by the school principal, Father Dunne (Norman McKay), who gently chastises the younger man, telling Father Clark that his place is at the school, working with his students, not doing something else, with an implied reference to Father Clark's work with the incarcerated and the formerly incarcerated. "If I thought you could be of better service someplace else, I'd be the first to tell you. [But] your job is here." The older priest reminds his younger colleague about the parent-teacher meeting that evening, but Father Clark begs off, saying that he has something else very important he must do.

That night in a burlesque bar, Father Clark meets with a waitress, Genny (Kelly Stephens). He presents her with a ticket and tells her where to meet her husband, who's being released from prison. When she questions if they can "make a go of it" after six years apart, the priest encourages her, telling her that "Charlie's a good man."

The priest encounters Billy and Pio in the back room of that same bar, where Billy is throwing dice and winning some cash. But his mounting winning is concerning the guys running the craps table, so one of them switches dice and starts a fight to bring the game to a halt. The cops arrive and drag Billy away on a charge of assault, but Father Clark is on the case. He pursues Louis Rosen (Larry Gates), one of the top criminal defense attorneys in St. Louis, to defend the young man. Rosen tries to put off the priest, saying that his retainer is $1,000, but Father Clark will have none of that, pointing out that he's a Jesuit priest and has taken a vow of poverty. But still he wants the attorney to represent Billy. Finally, Rosen agrees. In court, cross-examining a prosecution witness who claimed Billy started the fight, Rosen tricks the man into mentioning the gambling, and his boss blurts out that Billy didn't start the fight, after all — that it is his man who is really at fault.

Outside the courtroom, while Father Clark is impressing upon Billy the importance of his finding a legitimate job, they are approached by George McHale (Logan Ramsey), of the fictional St. Louis Times-Herald. The newspaperman wants to make the clergyman famous as "the hoodlum priest" who helps those in trouble with the law, but Father Clark declines the offer, not really wanting publicity. But because the priest shuns him, the reporter decides that if he can't write a story promoting the priest's efforts, then he will expose Father Clark as an accomplice in the crimes with those he has been helping. And he subsequently causes the priest a good deal of trouble. Immediately after his failed efforts to get a story out of Father Clark, McHale turns to the assistant district attorney (Vince O'Brien) and points out: "It's one thing to have Louie Rosen against you, but you've got God against you, too." Then he suggests that perhaps the priest may be complicit in crime with his associates.

But Father Clark is concentrating on finding young Billy a job. At first, they are met with a lot of "no's." Then the priest turns to produce merchant Angelo Mazzioti (Lou Martini) who instantly offers the young man work. "He's with you — what more I gotta know?" the other man asserts; he calls over his brother, Mario (Sam Capuano), and tells him to find something for Billy to do. But the brother apparently resents the young man from the beginning and appears ready to make it hard on his new worker.

The so-called "hoodlum priest" has decided that the time has come for inmates returning to St. Louis to have a "halfway house," where they can live while getting re-acclimated to society, so he turns to Louis Rosen for assistance. Rosen helps him put together a meeting of the most charitable rich women in town, and Father Clark explains his plan to the group. In the meantime, Billy is wandering around the grounds where the get-together is being held, and he meets Ellen Henley (Cindi Wood), whose mother is attending the function. She is immediately attracted to the handsome young man, and subsequently looks him up at work at the produce company and asks him to meet her for dinner afterward. Mario comes upon them and is upset that this ex-con could be going out with an attractive young woman of wealth.

Meanwhile, when Father Clark goes to the jail to meet with his "parishioners," he is barred from entry by order of the assistant district attorney. Now, the priest is brought before a civil board investigating whether or not he is complicit in criminal activity, as a result of information supplied by the newspaperman, McHale. He's defended at the hearing by his friend Louis Rosen, but it's actually Father Clark's own impassioned plea that convinces the Jesuit observer, Father David Michaels (Walter L. Wiedmer), that Father Clark should be relieved of his teaching duties entirely — so that he can devote full time to helping inmates and released prisoners. The civil authorities likewise decide not to pursue the case against Father Clark.

So plans move forward in establishing the halfway house for released cons, and, all the while, Billy and Ellen are falling in love. But all isn't rosy in River City. At work, Billy is called to the office where Angelo and Mario are present, along with a private investigator, and Mario charges that some meat has been stolen from the company. When Billy is questioned, he's reluctant to say that's he was out the previous even with Ellen, for fear that it might get her into trouble. Consequently, Mario gets his wish, and Billy is fired.

That night, Billy and Pio slip back into the produce company office, and Pio proceeds to drill into the safe while Billy keeps watch. Mario comes into the building and hears the drilling upstairs. When he enters the office, he finds Pio at the safe and attacks the intruder. Billy enters with a gun and tells Mario to back off. With attention off him, Pio flees the scene and Billy gets into a fight with Mario. When Billy also tries to leave, Mario attacks him again and, during the scuffle, is shot.

Billy then flees, with the police in hot pursuit. Pio calls Father Clark, who hurries over to an abandoned building where the police have Billy cornered. The police are reluctant to let the priest enter the building, but he breaks away from them and goes inside anyway. After a long discussion with Billy, he finally gets the young man to surrender his gun and leads him outside to the police.

Billy's trial results in a guilty verdict in the death of Mario Mazzioti, and a death sentence. Ellen comes to Billy in prison, confessing her love, and Father Clark tries frantically to get the death sentence overturned, even going to the governor, to no avail. Finally, he attends the doomed man in his waning moments as Billy is led away to the gas chamber.

After the execution, a despondent Father Clark walks back in the pouring rain to the half-completed halfway house. When Pio enters the building, the stunned priest can only watch as the drunken friend of the executed Billy Lee Jackson goes on a rampage and trashes a dormitory room. Afterward, when Pio collapses, exhausted and unconscious, the priest picks him up and places him on a bed to rest.

Tears form in Father Clark's eyes as the camera pans back and these words of conclusion appear on the screen: "On May 16th 1959, out of deep despair, a new hope was born with the opening of Dismas House."

Dismas is the name that the Catholic Church has traditionally given to the thief who hung beside Jesus on the cross and who admitted his guilt while declaring Jesus guiltless. It seems appropriate that this — which was also Father Clark's middle name — would be chosen for St. Louis' first halfway house for released prisoners.

And *The Hoodlum Priest*, while not being a glorious name for the film, is, nevertheless, a serious examination of a social problem that persists, not only in St. Louis but across the nation, almost a half-century after this movie was completed.

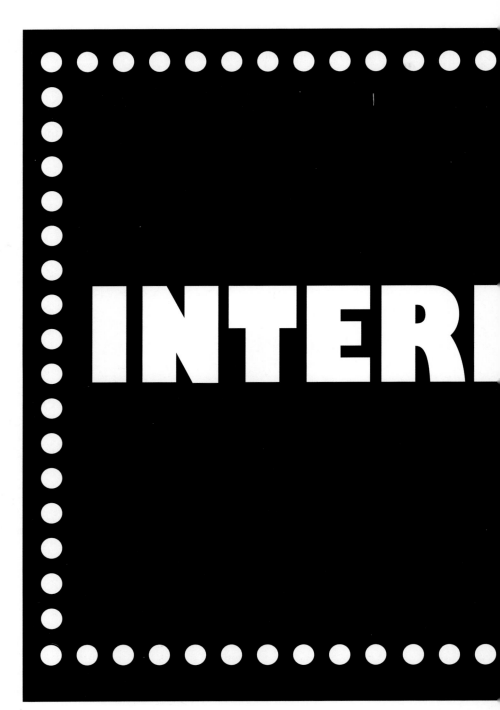

ISSION

Fox Theatre, 1929 (courtesy *West End Word*)

Did You Know...?

...that **Redd Foxx** was the only entertainer invited to Elvis Presley's wedding on May 1, 1967, at Las Vegas' Aladdin Hotel?

...that **Virginia Mayo**, widely considered to be one of the most beautiful actresses ever to grace the screen, was always filmed from a very careful perspective because she was slightly cross-eyed?

...that Jimmy Stewart was almost twice as old as the character he was playing, Charles A. Lindbergh, in **The Spirit of St. Louis**?

...that **John Goodman**'s first TV part was in a Burger King commercial in which he didn't speak and simply bit into a Whopper?

...that **Agnes Moorehead** had refused an offer to play Endora on *Bewitched* until she saw Elizabeth Montgomery at a department store, and Elizabeth asked her to reconsider?

...that Don Murray, who co-produced and starred in **The Hoodlum Priest,** also co-wrote the screenplay under the name Don Deer?

...that **Buddy Ebsen** was a staunch Republican who helped defeat his *Beverly Hillbillies* co-star Nancy Kulp when she ran as a Democrat for Congress, calling her "too liberal"?

...that although several members of the Smith household sing the title tune in **Meet Me in St. Louis** in the opening scene of the film, supposedly in 1903, in reality the song wasn't published until 1904?

...that the white streak in **Scott Bakula**'s hair actually first appeared when he was only four years old, and that his mother initially thought it was from paint because he had been playing at the house of a neighbor who was painting?

...that Fox Studios insured **Betty Grable**'s legs for more than a million dollars in 1943; hence, she became known as "the girl with the million-dollar legs"?

…that although **Parenthood** is clearly set in the metropolitan St. Louis area, the city's name is not mentioned once during the film?

…that **Kevin Kline** has played presidents in two different films, *Wild Wild West* (President Ulysses S. Grant) and *Dave* (fictional President Bill Mitchell)?

…that the promotional "tag" line for **The White Palace** was "the story of a younger man and a *bolder* woman"?

…that **Agnes Moorehead** was a teacher and oratory coach in Soldiers Field, Wisconsin, and her oratory team garnered a stack of trophies in competition with other schools while she was their coach?

…that Darryl Hickman, who had second billing in **Fighting Father Dunne**, also had an uncredited speaking role in *Meet Me in St. Louis* and is the older brother of Dwayne Hickman, who played the title role in the 1959-63 TV series, *The Many Loves of Dobie Gillis*?

…that **Robert Guillaume** suffered a stroke while acting in the TV series, *Sports Night*, and he returned to the show after a brief absence, playing a character recovering from stroke?

…that **The Big Brass Ring** was written by Orson Welles as the "bookend" to his famous *Citizen Kane* film, made at the start of his motion picture career (in 1941), but *Brass Ring*'s screenplay wasn't turned into a film until 14 years after his death?

…that **Vincent Price** was so superstitious that he often jokingly said that he had a crucifix, horseshoe, and mezuzah hung on his front door?

…that many of the characters that **Shelley Winters** played in her most significant films have died or were murdered (for example: *A Place in the Sun, The Night of the Hunter, Lolita, A Double Life, The Diary of Anne Frank, The Poseidon Adventure*)?

…that the wedding reception for the character Gino in **The Game of Their Lives** had three of the actual members from the 1950 team that beat England

DeBar Theater (from the *Globe-Democrat* Collection at the St. Louis Mercantile Library, University of Missouri–St. Louis)

St. Louis drive-in theatre (From the *Globe-Democrat* Collection at the St. Louis
Mercantile Library, University of Missouri-St. Louis)

in the World Cup games — the real Gino Pariani, plus Frank Borghi and Harry Keough, as well as members of their families — playing guests at the reception?

…that **John Goodman** has played both the President of the United States (on TV's *The West Wing*) and the King of England (in the film, *King Ralph*)?

…that **Phyllis Diller** has appeared as a solo pianist with more than 100 symphony orchestras across the nation?

…that **Scott Bakula** is the only actor who appears twice in "*TV Guide*'s 25 Legends of Sci-Fi" because of his lead roles in both *Quantum Leap* and *Star Trek: Enterprise*?

…that much of ***Chuck Berry: Hail! Hail! Rock 'n' Roll*** was filmed at St. Louis' Fabulous Fox — in which Chuck Berry performed in a 1987 concert celebrating his 60th birthday — in a theater where he wasn't permitted even to buy a ticket to attend a performance when he was growing up?

…that **Virginia Mayo**, whose real name was Virginia Clara Jones, took her stage name from a vaudeville act in which she performed with two men who called themselves the Mayo Brothers?

…that when he was young, **Redd Foxx** worked as a dishwasher and went by the name "Chicago Red" so as not to be confused from his friend "Detroit Red" — a man who like Redd Foxx, who had another name later in life, "Malcolm X"?

…that Mae West's film ***That St. Louis Woman*** (also known as *Belle of the Nineties*) was actually written by Mae West, and so were eight of the other dozen films she made in her career?

…that **Kevin Kline** turned down the title role in 1989's *Batman*?

…that **Betty Grable** was the highest paid woman in America in 1946 and '47 with an annual income of more than $300,000?

…that both Halle Berry and Whitney Houston were "also rans" for the role of Tina Turner in **What's Love Got to Do With It?** and that Laurence Fishburne only accepted the role of Ike Turner (after declining the part five times) when he learned that Angela Bassett would be playing Tina?

…that, in the 1970s, **Vincent Price** had his own book club specializing in mystery novels and called, what else, "Vincent Price Books"?

…that **Phyllis Diller**'s first appearance on nationwide TV was as a contestant on Groucho Marx's *You Bet Your Life* in 1950?

…that **Robert Guillaume** was the first African American to play the lead in *The Phantom of the Opera* musical?

…that "Dizzy" Dean's real name was not Jerome Herman Dean, as he told people in **The Pride of St. Louis**, but Jay Hanna Dean?

…that **Shelley Winters** was the roommate of Marilyn Monroe early in their careers?

…that the actual St. Louis police officers who thwarted the theft in **The Great St. Louis Bank Robbery** played themselves in the 1959 film?

…that one of the choruses of "We're Off to See the Wizard" in the *The Wizard of Oz* has **Buddy Ebsen**'s voice because it was recorded before he had to give up playing the Tin Man as a result of an allergic reaction?

The mighty Wurlitzer at the Fox Theatre (courtesy *West End Word*)

FEATURE

Chuck Berry: Hail! Hail! Rock 'n' Roll
1987

Directed by Taylor Hackford

Primary Cast:

Chuck Berry	*Himself*
Ingrid Berry	*Herself*
Eric Clapton	*Himself*
Robert Cray	*Himself*
Bo Diddley	*Himself*
Don Everly	*Himself*
Phil Everly	*Himself*
Mark Hale	*Himself*
Etta James	*Herself*
Johnnie Johnson	*Himself*
Steve Jordan	*Himself*
Bobby Keys	*Himself*
Chuck Leavell	*Himself*
John Lennon	*Himself*
Julian Lennon	*Himself*
Jerry Lee Lewis	*Himself*
Little Richard	*Himself*
Roy Orbison	*Himself*
Keith Richards	*Himself*
Linda Ronstadt	*Herself*
Joey Spampinato	*Himself*
Bruce Springsteen	*Himself*

Lots of people think of Chuck Berry as the father of Rock 'n' Roll music, and *Chuck Berry: Hail! Hail! Rock 'n' Roll* goes a long way toward

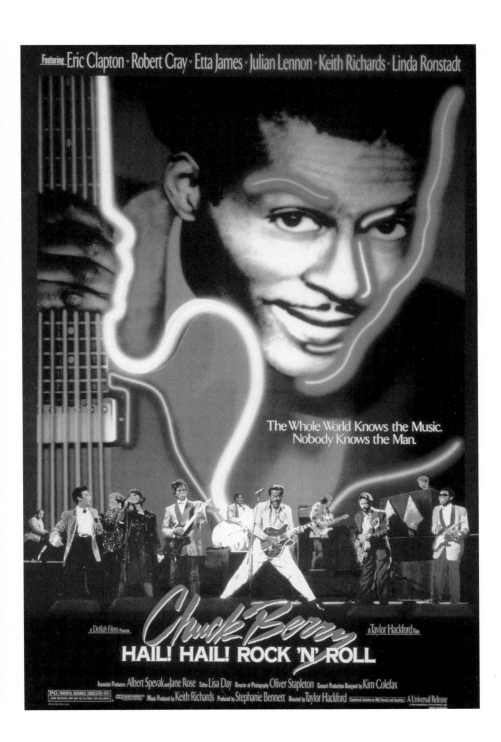

cementing that conclusion.

A combination documentary/biography/concert film, this production was filmed primarily at St. Louis' Fox Theatre during the 60th birthday concert by Chuck Berry that was presented there.

"If you had tried to give Rock 'n' Roll another name, you might call it Chuck Berry. Right! In the 1950s a whole generation worshipped his music, and when you see him perform today, past and present all come together, and the message is 'Hail! Hail! Rock 'n' Roll' Right on!"

That's the way the film opens, with this statement by John Lennon in tribute to Chuck Berry and his major contribution to rock 'n' roll music. The interesting thing about that testimonial is this: *Chuck Berry: Hail! Hail! Rock 'n' Roll* was made in 1987 on the occasion of Chuck Berry's 60th birthday, but John Lennon had died by an assassin's bullet some seven years previously. It just goes to show that Lennon and many others had long been cognizant of Chuck Berry's major contribution to the art form known as rock 'n' roll.

Then, with the title credit rolling, we see Chuck Berry singing his classic hit "Maybellene." Although no longer a young man, Chuck is still very much "into" his song, with the sweat glistening over his face. And this is followed by the first of many testimonials about how significant Chuck Berry's contribution to rock 'n' roll has been over the years. Both Little Richard and Bo Diddley offer their praises to the man whom they say set the pace for others to come over the following decades. These two are soon replaced on screen by the Everly Brothers, Phil and Don, who discuss hearing Chuck's music when they were young.

"He's the king of rock 'n' roll. My mama even said that." Another testimonial, and this one by none other than Jerry Lee Lewis, who himself was a major contributor to the music that originated in 1950s America. "And I said: 'What about me, Mama?' [And she said,] 'Well, Son, you vary. You're different. You sing slow songs.... But Chuck Berry is rock 'n' roll.' And I said, 'Well, all this time, I thought I was!' [And she replied,] 'Well, now you and Elvis are pretty good, but you're no Chuck Berry!'"

And from Little Richard: "My favorite song from Chuck is all of 'em!"

Next, Chuck drives up in his Cadillac to a dilapidated, now closed facility formerly known as the "Cosmopolitan Club." He declares. "Birthplace of 'Maybellene'!" Inside the former club, Chuck talks about the start of his career at this club "back in '51-52" and how he made $21 each weekend as a member of the Johnnie Johnson Trio. Then, as Johnnie Johnson himself notes on camera, Chuck came to him and asked about changing the name to the Chuck Berry Trio, and Johnnie told him that he had no problem with that. "It was perfectly okay with me because Chuck was more of a go-getter, and he seemed to know more about the business than I did. I figured with him as the leader, we would have more jobs and a better success."

Chuck points out that entertaining wasn't his primary source of income during those days. No, he worked with his father and at an automobile factory, where he made $91 a week. "Music was a sideline. I was a carpenter and a painter." After he'd been performing at the Cosmo Club in East St. Louis for about a year, he convinced the owners to let him paint the facility, and he created a mural of snow-capped mountains around the walls. "I got $450 for that, and compared to $21 a weekend, that's like six months of playing." He notes that he didn't give up painting as a source of income for some time. "Oh, when the money got larger, I put the paintbrush down, picked the pick up and fiddled." When he left the Cosmo Club, he started playing in Cleveland for $800 a week. "Then I found out you make more and more and more as the years go by."

Chuck also discusses making his first recordings and seeing the music sheets of his songs that also listed two other names besides his, not understanding why their names appeared on his songs, and later learning that it was part of what he calls "payola." Back in those days, as Bo Diddley and Little Richard note, the recording artist received only one-half of a cent per record.

We follow Chuck through Lambert Airport as he explains that he has developed a technique of doing "one-nighters; that's all I do: one nighters." He would travel along to his destination, where he would be backed up by a local band that was familiar with his "greatest hits." It was a Chuck Berry technique that he developed, notes his agent, Dick Alen: "This is Chuck Berry. That's all, Chuck Berry, doing it his way." Then we ride with Chuck on his plane as he explains more about his concert style, followed by his arrival and meeting with one of these local bands.

Now, one of those band leaders discusses what it was like to back up Chuck Berry, that it was as an experience he can tell his grandkids someday, and this guy has become something of a name in the music field himself — Bruce Springsteen! But still, he recalls fondly when he was in his early twenties, playing as a member of the backup band to Chuck Berry on one of these "one-nighters."

Chuck then takes us to his Berry Park that he created in St. Louis, with its own lake and its club, where in the 1960s he held music festivals that were attended by as many as 60,000 fans.

Now the film cuts to a rehearsal for Chuck's 60th birthday concert. Among those preparing for this event are Keith Richards of the Rolling Stones and Eric Clapton, and both talk about Chuck and what it's like to play with him — especially Keith Richards, who has lots to say about Chuck Berry and his music throughout the remainder of the film. During this rehearsal, we hear bits and pieces of classic Chuck Berry songs familiar to most of his fans.

Finally, it's on to the Fox Theatre, now empty, but it's just hours before the big concert. Chuck takes us inside and explains that, as a child, he couldn't even go inside this facility to see a film because of racism. Now, he's at the Fox as the main attraction!

On stage, Chuck Berry is ever the master showman. He sings all the songs that his fans have come to hear. There are such hits as: "Roll Over, Beethoven;" "Johnny B. Goode;" "Nadine;" "Back in the USA;" "Sweet Little Sixteen;" "No Money Down;" "Rock 'n' Roll Music;" "Too Much Monkey Business;" "Brown-Eyed, Handsome Man;" and "Wee Wee Hours," among others.

In addition to Keith Richards playing with him, Chuck is joined by several prominent guest singers including Linda Ronstadt, Robert Cray, Julian Lennon ("Look at him! Ain't he like his Pa? Yeah!" Chuck screams), Etta James, and Eric Clapton, each of whom individually sing along with Chuck on some of the rock 'n' roll hits he made famous back in the 1950s and '60s.

Sitting back after the concert is finished, Keith Richards makes the inevitable comparison of Chuck Berry with the Rolling Stones' lead singer: "He gives me more headaches than Mick Jagger, but I still can't complain. I love him, and I've done what I wanted to do for him. Now, I'm going to sleep for a month."

This film has been widely praised as one of the best combination biography and concert films; and, watching it, you can almost feel the electricity of the concert, but it's more than that. Despite Chuck's pretense that it's all about the money, it's obvious how much the man loves his music after a long lifetime of performing what several decades ago was referred to as "kids' music."

Inside the concert portion of the film are several comments by other famous musicians besides Keith Richards. Among these are Roy Orbison, who observes that Chuck Berry is the earliest example of the singer-songwriter in rock 'n' roll. Richards agrees, pointing out that there was no such creature before Chuck starting writing and performing his own songs in the 1950s.

And capping off the praise for Chuck Berry is perhaps this observation by John Lennon (from an interview in the 1970s): "His lyrics were very intelligent lyrics in the '50s. When people were singing virtually about nothing, he was writing social-comment songs" — and this perhaps the ultimate praise from a man who came to be known for his own musical observations about the state of mankind. "He was writing all kinds of songs with incredible meter to the lyrics, which influenced Dylan and me and many other people. He's the greatest rock 'n' roll poet; I really admire him."

Chuck Berry: Hail! Hail! Rock 'n' Roll is also obviously a labor of love from director Taylor Hackford, who shows his great admiration for the entertainer in this carefully crafted musical story of St. Louis' very own king of rock 'n' roll.

Virginia Mayo
Born November 30, 1920

Virginia Clara Jones was the great-great-great-granddaughter of the founder of East St. Louis — but she came to be known to the world as actress Virginia Mayo.

Born in St. Louis, Virginia began dance lessons at her aunt's studio when she was six. After she graduated from Soldan High School, she started her theatrical career as a dancer in her hometown at the Muny.

During the early years of her career as a performer, Virginia did a vaudeville act with two men in a horse costume. The men were known as the Mayo Brothers, hence Virginia's theatrical name was "born."

A strikingly beautiful woman, it was undoubtedly her physical attributes that piqued Samuel Goldwyn's attention when he saw her at a Broadway review. After he signed her to a contract with MGM, David O. Selznick was assigned to give her a screen test, which she "failed." But Goldwyn didn't give up on his St. Louis beauty, so he gave her a bit part in his 1943 film *Jack London*.

Also in 1943, Virginia got a walk-on part in *Follies Girl*. By the following year, she had graduated to better roles in the movies, playing Princess Margaret in *The Princess and the Pirate*, which also featured Bob Hope.

After that, she seemed to have steady work in film. Other '40s movies in which she appeared include *Up in Arms*; *Lady in the Death House*; *Seven Days Ashore*; *Three Men in White*; *Wonder Man*; *The Kid from Brooklyn*; *Out of the Blue*; *The Secret Life of Walter Mitty*; *Smart Girls Don't Talk*; *A Song is Born*; *Colorado Territory*; *The Girl From Jones Beach*; *White Heat*; *Red Light*; and *Always Leave Them Laughing*.

Her performance in *The Best Years of Our Lives* (1946) is considered one of the best from her early career. In it, she played Marie Derry, the faithless wife of Dana Andrews' character.

From the 1950s, some of her features included *Backfire*; *The West Point Story*; *Captain Horatio Hornblower RN*; *Painting the Clouds with Sunshine*; *Along*

Virginia Mayo at the Muny Opera Theatre (from the *Globe-Democrat* Collection at the St. Louis Mercantile Library, University of Missouri–St. Louis)

the Great Divide; Starlift; She's Back on Broadway; South Sea Woman; Devil's Canyon; King Richard and the Crusaders; The Silver Chalice; Pearl of the South Pacific; Great Day in the Morning; The Proud Ones; Congo Crossing; The Big Land; and The Story of Mankind.

After the '50s, Virginia did most of her performing on the legitimate stage and didn't appear in many motion pictures, with a total of only 13 films in the 1960s, '70s, and '90s (she didn't make any films in the '80s, although she did appear in the role of Peaches DeLight in the television series Santa Barbara in 1984). Among her movie appearances during these decades were Jet Over the Atlantic; McGarry and His Mouse; Young Fury; Castle of Evil; Fort Utah; Fugitive Lovers; French Quarter; The Haunted; Evil Spirits; Midnight Witness; and her last film appearance, 1997's The Man Next Door.

Virginia Mayo died on January 17, 2005, in Thousand Oaks, California, at the age of 84.

Parenthood
1989

Directed by Ron Howard

Written by Lowell Ganz, Babaloo Mandel, and Ron Howard

Primary Cast:

Gil Buckman	Steve Martin
Karen Buckman	Mary Steenburgen
Helen Buckman-Lampkin Bowman	Dianne Wiest
Frank Buckman	Jason Robards
Nathan Huffner	Rick Moranis
Tod Higgins	Keanu Reeves
Julie Buckman-Lampkin Higgins	Martha Plimpton
Garry Buckman-Lampkin	Leaf Phoenix (Joaquin)
Larry Buckman	Tom Hulce
David Brodsky	Dennis Dugan
George Bowman	Paul Linke
Susan Buckman Huffner	Harley Jane Kozak
Marilyn Buckman	Eileen Ryan
Grandma	Helen Shaw
Kevin Buckman	Jasen Fisher
Taylor Buckman	Alisan Porter
Justin Buckman	Zachary La Voy
Patty Huffner	Ivyann Schwan
Cool Buckman	Alex Burrall

STEVE MARTIN
TOM HULCE · RICK MORANIS · MARTHA PLIMPTON · KEANU REEVES
JASON ROBARDS · MARY STEENBURGEN · DIANNE WIEST

The director of "SPLASH,"
"WILLOW" and "COCOON"
brings you a comedy
about life, love and the gentle
art of raising children.

A RON HOWARD Film
Parenthood

It could happen to you.

IMAGINE ENTERTAINMENT Presents A BRIAN GRAZER Production "PARENTHOOD" Music by RANDY NEWMAN Costumes Designed by RUTH MORLEY
Film Editors MICHAEL HILL · DANIEL HANLEY Production Designer TODD HALLOWELL Director of Photography DONALD McALPINE, A.S.C. Executive Producer JOSEPH M. CARACCIOLO
Story by LOWELL GANZ & BABALOO MANDEL & RON HOWARD Screenplay by LOWELL GANZ & BABALOO MANDEL Produced by BRIAN GRAZER
PG-13 PARENTS STRONGLY CAUTIONED Some Material May Be Inappropriate for Children Under 13 Soundtrack Album Available on Warner Bros. Records, Cassettes and CDs. Directed by RON HOWARD A UNIVERSAL RELEASE

STEREO
ON VIDEOCASSETTE
COMING SOON ON LASER VIDEODISC
MCA HOME VIDEO

Young Gil Buckman	Max Elliott Slade
Lou	*Clint Howard*
Usher	*Lowell Ganz*

There can be no more demanding or more rewarding task than being a parent. In *Parenthood*, there are plenty of laughs (after all, this *is* a Steve Martin film), but these are secondary to the challenges presented to the extended Buckman family and the responsibilities of lifelong parenting.

When the story opens, it's the fourth inning of a St. Louis Cardinals game (probably in the early 1960s), and a man enters with his son, who appears to be about 10. The boy is complaining about coming in late to the game. As soon as the man has his son seated, he walks over to an usher and pays the man to watch his son until he gets back. The usher (screenwriter Lowell Ganz) sits down beside the boy, young Gil Buckman (Max Elliott Slade), who starts speaking to him in very sophisticated adult language. When the usher points out that the boy doesn't "talk like a kid," the youngster replies: "Yeah, I'm not really a kid. I'm a memory of when I was a kid. I'm 35 now. I have kids of my own…. I swore things would be different with my kids. It's my dream: strong, happy, confident kids…."

And that sets the stage for this very rewarding film. A few seconds later, the "kid" evolves into Steve Martin, as the adult Gil Buckman, who, along with his wife, Karen (Mary Steenburgen), is attending a modern Cardinals game with all three of their young children. After the Cardinals game ends, the family walks to their minivan, loaded with all sorts of Cardinals souvenir paraphernalia, and drives to their home in the suburbs. In the background, with the opening credits playing, we hear Randy Newman singing his Oscar-nominated song, "I Love to See You Smile."

Once the family arrives home, we get to see Gil interacting briefly with each of his children. The oldest, Kevin (Jasen Fisher), who's almost 9, has fallen asleep on the way back from the Cardinals game, so Gil gently carries the boy in and places him onto his bunk bed. The youngest, Justin (Zachary La Voy), who's about three, silently watches his dad and his older brother, and his father talks quietly to him. Then Gil finds his daughter, Taylor (Alisan Porter), in his bed sick, and she throws up over him. Later, after all three of the children are finally asleep, Gil and Karen are in bed kissing, and

Karen brings up that Kevin's principal wants the two of them to come in to see her about their son because of his emotional condition. There's also a brief discussion of their children compared to Gil's sister's offspring…

…Which is a segue into Gil's extended family. We meet his sister, Helen (Dianne Wiest) — in her role that also prompted an Oscar nomination — and her two children, Garry (Joaquin Phoenix, who's billed as Leaf Phoenix in the credits) and Julie (Martha Plimpton). Almost immediately, we realize how truly dysfunctional this family section is. Garry, who appears to be about 12, sulks out of his room (which he proceeds to padlock) carrying a mysterious paper bag, hardly speaking to his mother. Despite her attempts to carry on a conversation, he grabs some food from the kitchen and leaves, carrying his bag and his skateboard. Then, Helen goes to her daughter's room, and we first meet Julie, who's about 17. Helen enters the room, pointing out that her family is coming over that evening and asking Julie if she's okay. "I thought I heard you moaning last night." Julie dismisses the comment, saying she had a stomach ache. After the mother leaves, Julie's boyfriend, Tod (Keanu Reeves in one of his first film roles that indicated his potential as actor), climbs out from under the bed. "Man, your mother can talk," he asserts and proceeds to get dressed. But he stops to kiss Julie. Then, holding up a camera, he declares: "We can record our love."

Next, we move on to Gil's other sister, Susan (Harley Jane Kozak), and her husband, Nathan (Rick Moranis). We see Nathan speaking to someone unseen about how she can do better and shouldn't need to attend an "ordinary" university. Susan sits down beside her husband, also encouraging the unseen party to give that "extra effort." Now the camera pans to the other side of the room, and we see the object of this conversation, three-year-old Patty (Ivyann Schwan), who replies with, "Okay, Mama."

Later that day, we get to see the whole family in a gathering at Helen's home. We also meet Gil's parents. There's Frank (Jason Robards), whom we realize immediately isn't much better at parenting than he was when he abandoned his son at the Cardinals game with the usher, and there's Marilyn (Eileen Ryan), who plays a mousy character in a role that isn't developed significantly in the film. We also meet Gil's never-employed brother, Larry (Tom Hulce, who was previously nominated for an Oscar for *Amadeus*), the youngest of Frank and Marilyn's four children, and then there's Larry's son, Cool (Alex Burrall), whose mother is African American. Finally, there's

Grandma (Helen Shaw), who doesn't have much to say in the movie, but when she does, it's usually something funny or wise — and sometimes it's both.

So, there you have it. This is the Buckman family, all of whom are introduced and their characters basically defined in the first 20 minutes of the film.

Gil and Karen go to the meeting with Kevin's principal, who suggests that Kevin has emotional issues that they aren't prepared to deal with in the ordinary classroom, so she suggests they consider enrolling their son in special education classes. Gil immediately goes into denial, but they finally decide they'll send Kevin to a therapist.

Cut to Tod and Julie picking up the photos of their lovemaking. Only when they excitedly open the envelope, the pictures are from her mother's promotion at work. Julie tells the photo booth attendant that these are the wrong Buckman photos, but he explains that the other envelope has already been picked up. Now, we see Dianne Wiest in her Oscar-nominated role of Helen, sitting in the living room looking over the pictures of Julie and Tod and making slight sounds and comments. When her daughter comes in, there is a confrontation, so Julie goes into her room and quickly packs her bag and leaves, saying she's going to live with Tod because they love each other. Helen then tells her to never come back, but as soon as Julie is out of the house, her mother yells after her affectionately, telling the daughter to let her know if she needs anything.

At Frank's home, where Larry and Cool are staying for a while, the father is showing off his antique car, which he has diligently restored. The father and son talk about trivia, but it's evident how much Frank cares for his youngest son. Larry is sufficiently awed by his father's car; then he uses the opportunity to hit his dad up for $2,000.

The movie continues to jump around from one portion of the family to another in what could be a confusing and disjointed jumble in the hands of a less-talented director, but Ron Howard makes everything flow together smoothly.

In other scenes, we see Nathan and Susan discussing how Nathan is concerned about Patty being around Gil's children because he doesn't want her to be exposed to others not serious about learning; Gil at work and upset at his boss (Dennis Dugan) for passing over him for what he considers a well-deserved promotion; Gil with an upset Kevin at a video arcade; and Frank with his grandson, Cool, showing off his antique car; then Larry being tossed out of a speeding limo in front of them.

Julie is brought home by the Kirkwood Police after she's picked up for panhandling. She breaks down, sobbing as her mother hugs her. Finally, she tells her mother that she left Tod after a fight over his wanting to race dragsters. Suddenly, Tod bursts in on them, and Julie starts telling him off before she runs out of the house. He runs after her and grabs her. Helen starts hitting Tod with the newspaper, screaming that he should "let her go!" But Tod replies: "Please, Mrs. Buckman; I love her." Then he reveals that they are married. Finally, he gets on his knees and begs Julie's forgiveness.

Next, we jump back to Gil with Kevin, whom he's coaching in Little League. When Gil puts his son on second base, Kevin misses a fly ball, allowing the other team to score the winning run — to the dismay of the various parents in attendance, the most vocal of whom is played by Ron Howard's brother, Clint Howard, who often has small roles in Ron's films. This portion of the movie also continues to contrast fantasy visions of Steve Martin's character. First, when he watches his son playing ball, the pride swells inside him, and he sees a grown-up Kevin as valedictorian of class, thanking his father for helping him get through childhood. Then, later, after Kevin gets upset at his dad for "making me play second base," he sees a crazed, grown-up Kevin as a sniper shooting at people from the rooftops.

In other scenes, we see a disgusted Nathan upset at Susan for deliberately punching holes in her diaphragm; Julie and Tod now living in Helen's home and cutting each other's hair in punk designs; and Garry telling his mother that he thinks maybe he should go live with his dentist father, but being rejected when he calls his dad and asks him about it.

Some of the funniest portions of the film take place at Kevin's ninth birthday party. Gil has scheduled a St. Louis-area balloon-twisting, "cowboy" party entertainer to come to the event, but a stripper shows up instead. When she calls the booking office, she reports there's been a mistake —that Cowboy Dan went where she was supposed to have gone and was subsequently beaten up by the guys who had been expecting the stripper. Kevin overhears his parents discussing that Cowboy Dan won't make it to the party, and the boy gets very upset, whereupon Gil reassures his son that "Cowboy Dan is coming." Shortly thereafter, Gil shows up before the kids in one of the most hilarious makeshift cowboy outfits I've ever seen. At first, the kids mock him as just Kevin's dad, but soon Gil wins them over with his hysterical hijinks. That night, when he tucks his son into bed, Kevin asks Gil if, when he grows up, he can work where Gil works so they can "see each other all the time."

Following this scene of contentment is one of anger and frustration. Following on the footsteps of his father's refusing to let him come to live with him, Garry breaks into the man's dental office and smashes up the place with a hammer. After that, Helen breaks the lock on her son's room and goes inside, whereupon she finds the infamous paper bag and, inside it, sex films. When Garry comes in, he's very upset that his mother has broken into his private domain, but she tells him that his hammer was found at the scene of destruction at his father's clinic. While they're talking, Tod comes into Garry's room, and Helen bends over and whispers something in Tod's ear. Some time later, Tod comes out of the boy's room, and he tells Helen that her son is just learning to deal with his pubescent sexuality (but not in such clinical terms).

Frank finds that his antique car is missing from his garage; Kevin is bullied by other kids at the video arcade, and they take his money; Kevin becomes hysterical after he loses his retainer, and his parents try in vain to find it in the trash outside; and Gil crashes the minivan after Karen performs oral sex on him in the vehicle to try and relieve his tension.

When Frank drives up, he sees Larry returning his antique car to the garage, and Larry offers a tale about taking the car for appraisal, which he can't get because he doesn't have the papers. Frank becomes very angry and starts shouting at his youngest son, saying he knows that Larry was trying to sell his car. That's when Larry breaks down and admits that he has large gambling debts and that his debtors are going to kill him if he doesn't come up with $26,000.

Nathan is still working with Patty, showing her flash cards, when his wife shows up with some flash cards of her own, announcing that she's leaving him; Helen goes out on a date with biology teacher George Bowman (Paul Linke); Julie and Tod have another confrontation over his wanting to race dragsters, and he leaves; Julie tells her mother and the biology teacher that she's pregnant; Gil quits his job after his boss still refuses to give him a partnership in the firm; and, afterward, Karen tells him that she, too, is pregnant.

As Gil is preparing for another Little League game to start, Frank goes to see his oldest son for advice about how to deal with his youngest son because, as he puts it, he was always a bad father, while Gil is a good father. But mostly Frank talks to himself about the problem with Larry.

On the other end of the father-and-son spectrum, at the end of the Little League game, Gil's team needs only one more out, but Clint Howard's character is afraid that Kevin will "blow" another game, so he tells his son to field any ball anywhere that he can. When a fly ball is hit high in the air right toward Kevin, the other boy moves to catch it as well, knocking it out of Kevin's glove in a collision, but Kevin makes another lunge for the ball and catches it before it hits the ground. When this occurs, Gil becomes delirious with joy, dancing around the baseball diamond as only Steve Martin can.

At his home, Frank sits Larry down and explains how he'll pay off Larry's gambling debt a thousand dollars a month if Larry goes to work for him and attends Gamblers Anonymous. Larry agrees — then "adds a wrinkle," whereby he'll go to Chile for a month on another wild goose chase and then come back to work out Frank's deal. That's when the father realizes his youngest son will never change. Later, as Larry's packing to leave, Cool comes out on the porch where Frank is sitting, and the grandfather asks the boy if he'd like to stay with him. Cool nods his head and replies simply, "Yeah."

Nathan realizes he cannot stand living without Susan, so he goes to the school where she teaches and comes into her classroom singing, "Close to You." When she hugs and kisses him at the end of his serenade, the whole classroom bursts into applause.

At his first drag race, Tod crashes his brother's car, but Julie, Helen, and Garry are all there for support; Gil informs Karen that his boss called and begged him to come back to work, with a raise and a corner office; Gil's whole family goes to the school to see Taylor in her class play; and we hear Justin utter his first lines when he thinks someone in attacking his big sister on stage.

In the closing scene of the film, the entire extended family is sitting around a hospital waiting room waiting for a birth. Then George (the biology teacher, remember?) comes out and says that Helen and the baby are fine. Then we see that both Karen and Julie have already had their babies and that Susan is now expecting her second child. Everyone seems very happy as Frank hands out cigars, and, after taking down a "no smoking" sign, he lights up his own cigar, smiling broadly.

So, there you have it. *Parenthood* is a film that deals with the ins and outs of parenting from birth to old age. Overall, this is a very fine and rewarding film that shows how good a filmmaker Ron Howard has turned out to be long after he was Opie on *Andy Griffith* and Richie on *Happy Days*.

And this is definitely an interesting St. Louis story that shows us scenes around town, the hometown Cardinals, and even the Kirkwood Police without once even mentioning the city's name!

Redd Foxx
Born December 9, 1922

His parents called him John Elroy Sanford, and he went on to star as "Fred Sanford" in the long-running TV show *Sanford and Son*, but his stage name was Redd Foxx.

With a total of 135 episodes, *Sanford and Son* ran from 1972 through 1977. The series was based on a British series called *Steptoe and Son*. So, when the concept was developed for American television, with Redd Foxx in the title role, using his real last name was something of an inside joke.

Although Redd made very few films, *Sanford and Son* was not his first appearance before the camera. His first role was as Redd, the piano player, in the 1960 film *All the Fine Young Cannibals*, and he didn't show up again on screen for a decade — until 1970, when he played Uncle Bud in the cult classic, *Cotton Comes to Harlem*.

After *Cotton* came the TV role of Fred Sanford two years later, and, while that show was still in production, he did another comedy, in 1976, called *Norman...Is That You?* Then, after *Sanford and Son* completed its run, Redd was the main star of 1977-78 humorous variety television show, *The Redd Foxx Comedy Hour*.

In 1980, Redd tried to revisit his success with the TV series *Sanford*, a short-run show in which he reprised his role as Fred Sanford, this time minus his son, who had supposedly moved from Los Angeles to Alaska to work on the oil pipeline there. Without the give-and-take verbal banter between father and son, the show flopped. Another less than stellar success was the 1986 *Redd Foxx Show*, another sitcom, which lasted for only 12 episodes.

But Redd's broadcast career went on with a TV movie the following year, *Ghost of a Chance*. Then, in 1989, he played Bennie Wilson in the enjoyable theatrical film *Harlem Nights*, which also starred Richard Pryor and Eddie Murphy.

In 1991, Redd Foxx returned to series television with *The Royal*

Redd Foxx (from the *Globe-Democrat* Collection at the St. Louis Mercantile Library, University of Missouri–St. Louis)

Family, in which he co-starred with Della Reese as recent retirees, Al and Victoria Royal, who now have their newly divorced daughter and her three children living with them. The show started with very promising ratings after seven episodes, but Redd collapsed on the set during a rehearsal and later died, on October 11, 1991, in a Los Angeles hospital as a result of a heart attack.

Although he came to wide public attention because of his television and motion picture performances, Redd Foxx began his career and continued to appear as a stand-up comic from the 1940s throughout the remainder of his life. Redd was known for what some call "blue" humor, which emphasized sex, and largely was not accepted in the white community during the early years. However, among African Americans, he was highly appreciated for his sharp wit — something that translated readily to his Fred Sanford character, albeit somewhat "cleaned up" for wide audience consumption.

Redd Foxx was one of the few performers to star on television series on all three of the major broadcast television networks. Too bad there weren't more movies, but we can still appreciate those he did do.

White Palace
1990

Directed by Luis Mandoki
Written by Ted Tally and Alvin Sargent

Primary Cast:

Max Baron	James Spader
Nora Baker	Susan Sarandon
Neil	Jason Alexander
Edith Baron	Renee Taylor
Judy	Eileen Brennan
Rachel	Rachel Levin (Rachel Chagall)
Rosemary	Kathy Bates
Sol Horowitz	Steven Hill
Ella Horowitz	Hildy Brooks
Larry Klugman	Corey Parker
Sherri Klugman	Barbara Howard
Marv Miller	Jonathan Penner
Heidi Solomon	Kim Myers (Kim Meyers)
Sophie Rosen	Mitzi McCall
Janey	Maria Pitillo

You know you're in St. Louis from the opening scene of *White Palace*. There's James Spader driving along in his Volvo with the Arch dominating the background.

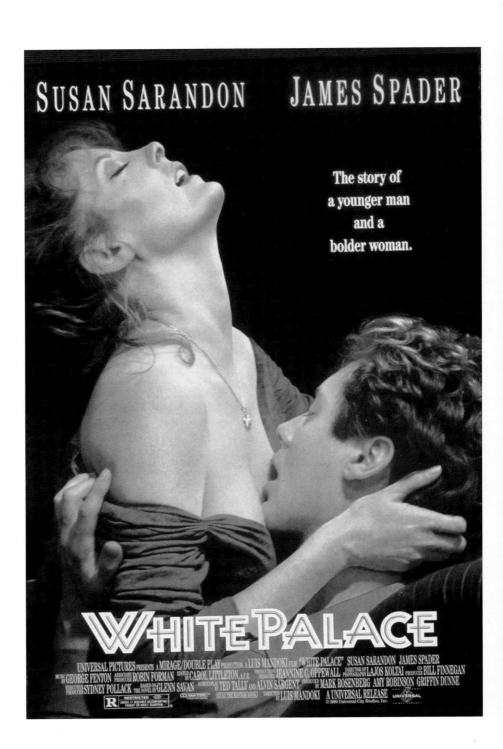

This is a film so obviously filmed and set in St. Louis that anyone who's ever lived in (or even visited) "River City" is bound to realize it. There are the landmarks: not only the Arch but also such things as the Fox Theatre and the well-known streets. There are also the references: comments about stores, locations, and area communities. And there's the attitude: At one point, Susan Sarandon makes a comment about a "dumb hoosier." Where else but St. Louis does the word "hoosier" carry such negative connotations? Certainly not in Indiana, and not even in outstate Missouri. "Hoosier," as St. Louisans use it, is definitely a one-town word.

So, at the beginning of this film, we see James Spader, who plays Max Baron, driving along in his Volvo, listening to classical music, seemingly content enough. He goes inside his expensive and antiseptically clean apartment and listens to his phone messages, then proceeds to change into his tuxedo, and he's off to the bachelor party for his friend Neil (Jason Alexander). All seems calm and quiet in Max Baron's life.

But, despite external appearances to the contrary, Max isn't really content with his existence. He's actually an emotional wreck. We get the first hint about his internal turmoil when Max arrives at the bachelor party. It seems he's been assigned to pick up the hamburgers at White Palace (not quite White Castle, but close — and this is another thing that says this film is a St. Louis story; many are the individuals who return "home" to St. Lou and have to get a taste of that hometown White Castle burger). When Max enters with his bags of burgers, one of the other guests discovers that six of the burger boxes are empty; this infuriates Max, who declares he's going back to White Palace to get the missing burgers — or his money back. No one else at the bachelor party (as well as those of us watching the film) can understand Max's frustration, especially Neil, who is the guest of honor. Neil urges his buddy to just forget it, but Max insists and piles into his Volvo yet again.

It is at the White Palace burger joint that we first meet Susan Sarandon's character, Nora. Max pushes himself to the front of the line of those waiting at the counter to order and confronts Nora, who's the cashier. They have a brief clash, during which he shows his indignation that he ended up with six empty boxes, and she asks how she can know he didn't just eat the burgers and bring the boxes back empty. But, finally, she opens the cash register and refunds Max's money.

Back at the bachelor party, Max enters as the group is looking at slides from their younger days, and the projector gets stuck on a photo of a young girl named Janey, whom Neil declares that Max dated from the time they were in kindergarten. But Max cannot stop staring at the image stuck on the screen. Later, as Max is preparing to drive home, Neil tells his friend that he has to move on beyond Janey and start dating again. After all, it has been two years.

On the way back to his apartment, Max stops at a honky-tonk bar, where he sits drinking, and a few seats away is Nora, who spots Max and remembers him from their little encounter. She walks over, plops down beside him, and begins a torrent of verbal comments designed to sexually arouse Max. But he seems oblivious to her advances. So she orders Max another drink and takes a more direct approach, getting in his face and placing her hand on his upper thigh; but he simply asks her to remove it. However, she doesn't back off, appearing to be both drunk and determined to get Max into bed. When Max doesn't relent, she begins to probe for other women in his life, and it becomes apparent that Janey still has a strong hold on his emotions.

When Max gets up to leave the bar, Nora declares that she's sorry that his other woman "dumped" him. That's when Max reveals that Janey didn't leave him — that she died in a car crash. At this point, Nora breaks into a sudden burst of uncontrolled, drunken laughter, and Max says that apparently no one close to her has ever died. But, still laughing, she remarks that Charlie did. "Who's Charlie? Your dog?" No, she responds, he was her "kid."

A few moments later, Max stumbles to his car, obviously now very wasted himself, and, as he's trying to start the engine, Nora taps on the passenger window and asks him to drive her home. Reluctantly, he agrees. After he runs over her mailbox and smashes one of the front lights on his Volvo, Nora insists that he'd better come inside so she can make him some coffee.

Once we enter Nora's house with Max, we realize how totally different her world is from his. The place is a filthy mess, with papers, cosmetics, and food scattered all over the place — in stark contrast to the sterile appearance of Max's apartment. When Nora goes for the coffee, there is none, so she offers Max another drink instead; but he declines and stumbles into her cluttered bathroom instead. When he emerges, Max declares that he's feeling sick and needs to lie down. So Nora puts him in her bed. But he is awakened by an image of his deceased wife, who begins to aggressively "attack" him sexually. It's soon obvious that the woman isn't Janey but Susan Sarandon's extremely eager character. What Nora does to Max would likely be called "date rape" were the sexes reversed in this encounter, although Max seems quite gratified by the experience. However, it appears to be just a "one-night stand." The next morning, when Nora asks if she's ever going to see him again, Max replies simply, "No," then walks out the door.

But it isn't that simple. Max can't get Nora out of his head, so, after work, he drives to White Palace and watches until she gets off work and climbs onto a bus for home. There, he knocks on her door, and when she answers, he's holding a shovel in his hands and announces that he has arrived to repair her demolished mailbox. But they both know that that isn't really why he's come back, so Nora tries to gently turn him away by contrasting their ages, pointing out that she's almost 44. He declares that he's 27, and then they lunge into each other's arms and onto the floor of her cluttered living room.

It's obvious from the beginning how different are the realities of Max Baron and Nora Baker. He's a young business executive who's well-educated and from an upper middle-class Jewish family. She's a middle-aged, low-income waitress from "the other side of the tracks" who was brought up Catholic. They seem to have little in common, except their lust for sex. Yet there appears to be an attraction beyond that.

This is definitely a story of "opposites attract" and also a bit of "the fish out of water." Clearly, Max doesn't seem to quite fit in Nora's "poor, white trash" world, and he is reluctant to try and bring her into his. He spends most of his free time hanging around her house and going to honky-tonk bars with her. His friends and even his mother want to know where he's disappeared to, leaving all manner of enticing messages on his answering machine. Even his boss (Kathy Bates) points out that he has started coming in late to work and is taking excessively long lunches, but she's gentle with Max, telling him simply to confine his sexual activity to his own time.

Despite Neil's urging for him to "bring a date" to his wedding, Max is hesitant to do so and even lies to Nora, telling her that he'll be at his mother's house, helping her with taxes. When Nora's electricity goes out because she hasn't paid her bill, she tries to reach him, getting his mother's phone number and calling her, only to find out where Max actually is. This leads to a confrontation, with Nora telling Max to never lie to her again. But Nora has begun to realize that Max may never let her into his upper middle-class domain.

Nora's older sister, Judy (Eileen Brennan), shows up at Nora's house from out of town while Max is there alone (Nora is working). Because she's psychic, she senses some of the tension in Max and Nora's relationship. Later, when Nora comes home, the three of them share some gentle moments together. It's obvious that Max feels an affinity for Judy. When she's preparing to leave, he walks her out and even kisses her goodbye after she gets into her jalopy for the drive back to New York City.

Soon after Judy's visit, Max decides to take Nora to his apartment and cook a fine meal for the two of them. However, in the grocery, while Nora is waiting for him at the checkout, Max encounters Neil's new wife, Rachel, who insists he come for Thanksgiving and bring his lady friend along. Nora sees him talking to Rachel in the distance and later asks about the conversation, so Max reluctantly proposes that Nora join him at the family get-together. That's when Nora becomes a fish out of water also, feeling very much out of place with Max's friends and family. After a couple of minor confrontations (which she provokes) during dinner, Nora stands up, announces that she's leaving and storms out.

Nora now believes that there is no long-term future for the two of them, that neither she nor Max can feel comfortable in the other's world. So she packs up and leaves town without announcing her intention. Max discovers the house abandoned but with a note from Nora asking him not to try and find her.

Afterward, Max is miserable. He tries seeing other women but realizes just how much he cares for his "older woman." After a period of wallowing in his sorrow, he heads for New York, where he locates Judy, who tells him where to find Nora working in a restaurant. When he enters the dining establishment, Nora insists that they have no future together, that she's never going back to St. Louis. At this point, Max announces that he isn't going back either, that he has quit his job and moved into a small New York apartment. He declares that he wants to be with her and that he *loves* her, bending her over a table and kissing her passionately as all the restaurant's patrons stare at the spectacle.

Stories about "mismatched" couples are nothing new in movies, and *White Palace* follows an often-used formula. Although this professes to be the tale of a "May-December" romance, it comes across as one driven more by lust than love. Even at the end, it's far from convincing that there's a strong bond of love between these two individuals.

Still, for residents of "River City" who'd like to see their hometown in the movies, this has plenty of local sites and "tastes" of St. Louis.

Robert Guillaume
Born November 30, 1927

Known the world over for his portrayal of the smart, tough, and witty butler who became a lieutenant governor in two television series of the 1970s and '80s, Robert Guillaume is also an accomplished singer and Broadway actor who has been nominated for, and won, numerous awards for his achievements as a performer. Then, in 1999, after he suffered a stroke in real life, his condition was written into the character he was playing on the sitcom *Sports Night*, and he returned to work after just a few weeks' absence.

Born in St. Louis and named Robert Williams, when he went into theater he decided to choose a name that he felt would be more distinctive. " 'Guillaume' is French for 'William,' and I just like the sound of it," he told me in 2002 when I interviewed him.

Robert grew up in downtown St. Louis and went to St. Nicholas Elementary School, St. Joseph High School, and St. Louis University, then later also to Washington University. He left the city in 1960, but he remembers as a child performing "in little school plays with the crepe paper tutus and the triangular hats."

It wasn't until he was in his mid-twenties, however, that he actually thought of becoming a performer, he contends. It was then "that I first thought that maybe I'd sing, and my original goal was to become a concert singer of German lieder [songs] and French art songs and that sort of thing. Then I sort of zeroed in on the Metropolitan Opera as a goal."

When he received a scholarship from Washington University to study in Aspen, Colorado, he "met some people from Cleveland who invited me to come there and go on the stage.

"I had always sung in those school plays, and I had some notion that I had talent," he added, modestly. "I went to New York and worked in a show called *Free and Easy*. That was my first paying job [as a performer]. I worked

Robet Guillaume (from the *Globe-Democrat* Collection at the St. Louis Mercantile Library, University of Missouri–St. Louis)

with Quincy Jones and a lot of the old jazz greats. He put together a jazz band, and we were doing *Free and Easy*, which was a rehash of an old Broadway show called *St. Louis Woman* that [had] starred Pearl Bailey in 1946." The company was supposed to tour Europe, then end up in London performing with Sammy Davis, Jr., but the show ran out of money, stranding the actors in Paris until Actors Equity came to their aid and brought them all back to New York.

Robert also did two cross-country tours of *Purlie* and is the only African-American to perform the lead in *The Phantom of the Opera*. He is especially proud of his work on stage in *Guys and Dolls*, which showcased an all African-American cast, and for which he was nominated for a Tony Award for his portrayal of Nathan Detroit. That was his last Broadway appearance, in 1976, "and a year later I got *Soap*, and I was in *Soap* from '77 to '79."

To many, Robert Guillaume is known for his breakout, strong-willed character, Benson DuBois, which he created in TV's *Soap* and later in the spin-off, *Benson*. But how much of the character's acerbic wit and self-assuredness was his interpretation of the role and how much was the writing? Modestly, he protests, "Well, I think most of it was in the writing," pointing out that the character was "written against type, meaning that the character was written to defy the type," or stereotype, that the audience might expect in an African-American butler in the 1970s. However, many feel that it took an assertive, self-assured performer like Robert to pull off the part successfully, a role for which he won a Best Supporting Actor Emmy for *Soap* and a Best Lead Actor Emmy for *Benson* — probably the only performer in the history of television to win both awards for playing the same character.

Before *Soap*, Robert was practically a television novice. "I had done an *All in the Family*, *Marcus Welby*, and an episode of *Julia* — but those were just guest shots," he points out. In the last three decades, however, he has come to like the medium, having performed in many television productions as well as motion pictures such as *Fire and Rain*, *Pandora's Clock*, *Super Fly TNT*, and as the voice of the mystical baboon Rafiki in Disney's animated blockbuster, *The Lion King*. "I think I prefer [performing] before the camera," he declares.

In 1979, he made *The Kid from Left Field*. Then, in the '80s, his motion picture career began in earnest with such films as *Seems Like Old Times*, *Prince Jack* (as Martin Luther King, Jr.), *They Still Call Me Bruce*, *Wanted: Dead or Alive*, and *Lean on Me*.

Then, in the 1990s, some of his films included *Death Warrant, The Meteor Man, Spy Hard, First Kid, Silicon Towers*, and then two voice interpretations of Rafiki in both *The Lion King* and *The Lion King II: Simba's Pride*.

Doing voices in cartoon features has boomed for Robert since 2000, with such films as *The Land Before Time VIII; The Big Freeze; The Adventures of Tom Thumb and Thumbelina; Extreme Sky Adventure; The Lion King 1½;* and *Half Life 2*. He appeared in the films *13th Child* in 2002 and *Big Fish* in 2003.

Robert Guillaume has also tried his hand working behind the camera. With his wife, Donna, he produced *You Must Remember This* for PBS and also *Happily Ever After*, a group of ethnically diverse fairy tales that he narrated for HBO.

In 1999, when he suffered that stroke while in his dressing room between takes for the sitcom *Sports Night*, he wasn't away from work for long. He returned in a matter of weeks, portraying a stroke survivor. But whose idea was that? "It was my wife's," he proclaims. "She thought of it and suggested the idea to the executive producer, that we might incorporate the stroke into the role; and, indeed, Aaron Sorkin did that, so I came back to the show as a real survivor of a stroke."

As the first African-American to play the lead in of *The Phantom of the Opera*, he experienced some resentment, but, Robert says, "I expected that. You see, that's the way I've always treated racism. In other words, racism never caught me off guard, I don't think, and it was my reaction to the possibility that was the secret of any success I would have."

What's Love Got to Do With It?
1993

Directed by Brian Gibson

Written by Tina Turner, Kurt Loder, and Kate Lanier

Primary Cast:

Tina Turner	*Angela Bassett*
Ike Turner	*Laurence Fishburne*
Darlene	*Khandi Alexander*
Zelma Bullock	*Jenifer Lewis*
Alline Bullock	*Phyllis Yvonne Stickney*
Young Anna Mae Bullock	*Rae'ven Kelly*
Choir Mistress	*Virginia Capers*
Grandma Georgiana	*Cora Lee Day*
Reggie	*Sherman Augustus*
Fross	*Chi McBride*
Spider	*Terrence Riggins*
Jackie	*Vanessa Bell Calloway*
Leanne	*Pamela Tyson*
Lorraine Taylor	*Penny Johnson*
Phil Spector	*Rob LaBelle*
Ike Turner, Jr.	*Richard T. Jones*
Michael Turner	*Shavar Ross*
Ronnie Turner	*Damon Hines*

Who needs
a heart
when
a heart
can be
broken ?

What's love got to do with it

The true life story of Tina Turner

Craig Turner	*Suli McCullough*
Young Ike Turner, Jr.	*Tyrandis Holmes*
Young Michael Turner	*Jamaine Harrington*
Young Ronnie Turner	*Devon Davison*
Young Craig Turner	*Eric E. Thomas II*
Ramada Inn Manager	*O'Neal Compton*

It all started in St. Louis — careerwise, that is — for Anna Mae Bullock. The world came to know Anna Mae as Tina Turner, and her story is one of both devastation and triumph, a story revealed in *What's Love Got to Do With It?*

Yes, this one is somewhat different from most of our "St. Louis movies." In this film, most of the story doesn't take place in St. Louis, but a critical part does, for St. Louis is where Ike and Tina lived when they met, and this was the starting point for a talent that blossomed over decades and is now known the world over.

The film opens in the mid-1940s in rural Tennessee. An African-American church choir is rehearsing "This Little Light of Mine," and the smallest choir member may well have the biggest voice. But she incurs the wrath of the choir director (Virginia Capers) for her rather flamboyant rendition of the gospel hymn, so she's sent out of the church.

This child, this very young Anna Mae Bullock (Rae'Ven Kelly), strolls down the dusty road and through the fields toward her home. Then, as she nears the residence, she hears some shouting, and a pickup speeds away. Inside the home a few minutes later, there is only Anna Mae until her grandmother arrives and takes her away on horseback.

The next scene takes place in St. Louis more than a decade later. It's 1958, and the 18-year-old Anna Mae (Angela Bassett) has arrived in the big city by bus. There to meet her is her mother (Jenifer Lewis) and sister, Alline (Phyllis Yvonne Stickney), and she goes to live with them. Her mother apologizes for missing her grandmother's funeral and also for leaving her with her grandmother to raise.

Right away, on the night of her arrival in St. Louis, her sister takes

Anna Mae to the club where she tends bar, and the music is provided by Ike Turner (Laurence Fishburne) and his band. At the end of each of his sessions, Ike had the tendency to pass the mike around to women who aspired to join his group, but no one seemed to live up to his expectations.

In the next scene, we see Anna Mae practicing her singing in the bathroom at home, where she is discovered by her sister and mother. Nevertheless, she dresses in a much more sophisticated and adult fashion this second night and goes back to the club. This time, when the mike is passed around, Anna Mae is prepared to show her stuff, and show it she does. Ike seems truly impressed.

Afterward, Ike takes her out to eat, and he tells her: "Anna Mae! Girl, you shocked the hell out of me. Where a little woman like you get such a big voice?" And he proceeds to tell her he wants her to join his ensemble.

Later on, she's so excited that she's bubbling over with joy when she tells her sister, but Alline calls her a "gullible country girl" who's in "the clouds." Nevertheless, a few moments later, a fancy convertible pulls up in front of the house, and Ike strolls in and tells her mother that he wants Anna Mae to sing with his group. At first, the mother resists, telling Ike that she wants her daughter to be a nurse "and bring in a steady paycheck." But Ike has an answer for that: "Mrs. Bullock, you ever see a nurse driving an automobile as fine as mine?" And that was it. All the two of them had to do after this comment was to discuss the details and for Ike to hand a little money over to the mother. "Put it like this: I can get anybody in St. Louis to sing in my band, but I want her," he concluded.

And so a career is born!

But from the very beginning, Ike is very demanding in what he wants out of Anna Mae. While she's rehearsing, he keeps telling her to sing "rougher...that's what sells records."

And that's what was to define their relationship over the next two decades — rough!

Ike decides to take the group with his new girl singer on tour, but just as with everything else, Ike is always in control.

From the first, Ike's girlfriend, Lorraine (Penny Johnson) is very jealous of Anna Mae, and she comes into where Anna Mae is sleeping brandishing a gun. But she says that the girl "ain't even worth the bullet" and goes into another room and shoots herself. Although she doesn't die, that is the end of her relationship with Ike, who has now turned his attention to Anna Mae.

The tour is a whirlwind of activity for the young Anna Mae Bullock, and she seems to be a hit wherever Ike Turner and the Kings of Rhythm go. But Ike is always demanding more and more of her. Then the inevitable happens. They have their first child. While she's lying in the hospital bed, the radio is playing, announcing "A Fool in Love" sung by Ike and Tina Turner, a stage name he had adopted for her without young Anna Mae having even been consulted. It was a name she resisted at first and, years later, fought desperately to keep.

Ike spirits his "Tina" out of the hospital, down the fire escape, because the doctor had said she was too exhausted to leave — typically he had to have it *his* way — and he takes her to Mexico, where they officially wed.

Before long, he has her back before the crowds, belting out songs he had written as well as those by other popular songwriters. Some of the now-familiar songs included in their tour repertoire include: "Rock Me Baby," "Shake a Tail Feather," "It's Gonna Work Out Fine," and "(Darlin), You Know I Love You."

After Ike and Tina's marriage, Lorraine shows up again and drops off the two sons that she had with Ike. He's very angry at her, and he chases after her as she drives away, asking, "What am I gonna do with two more kids?" But Tina takes the boys in as her own, and the family grows.

Financially, the Turners are prospering. They have hit after hit, and now, in the mid '60s, Ike moves his growing family to Hollywood. But all isn't a bed of roses at home. With luxury all around him, Ike just cannot be content, so he lashes out at Tina, physically beating her again and again. Even as family and friends tell her to stop, she continues to cover for him.

Still, Ike and Tina couldn't be more popular. Their records are selling like crazy, and they continue to tour and perform before sold-out audiences. Then, she is approached by famous producer Phil Spector (Rob LaBelle), who wants Tina to record with him. At first, Ike is very excited — until Spector tells Ike that he wants only Tina. But he doesn't try to stop her, and Tina records with a large symphonic orchestra. Even though Ike praises her work, it's obvious that he's jealous of his wife's success.

One day as they're dining out, Ike goes off the deep end, even threatening to beat up one of his backup singers, Jackie (Vanessa Bell Calloway), but she storms out of the restaurant, telling Tina: "You're a dead woman, if you stay here." Tina takes Jackie's admonition to heart, and that night, while Ike's asleep, she sneaks out with their children. She calls her mother and tells her she's coming home, asking her not to tell Ike. But, of course, her Mom does tell, so Ike chases his family down and takes them back home with him. Tina was to stay in the bondage of this abusive relationship for another decade before she finally made good on her escape.

By 1968, Ike and Tina Turner are a worldwide phenomenon, and they're not only performing all over the United States, but even in Europe. But now Ike's become a cokehead, and that even more complicates their relationship. Finally, Tina has just about reached her wit's end, and she overdoses on pills. She's rushed to the hospital, and, as she's recovering, Jackie comes for a visit. After Tina gets out of the hospital, she accepts Jackie's invitation to come to her house for a visit, and it's here that Jackie introduces her to Buddhism and Buddhist meditation. It's what turns her life around.

Finally, Tina finds the courage to fight back against Ike's abuses — literally. It happens while they're being driven by limo to a hotel: he starts hitting her, and she starts hitting back. When they march out of the vehicle into the hotel, they are both bruised and bloody. That night, she walks out without a cent in her pocket and goes to another hotel and asks for a room, explaining that she doesn't have any money but that she will pay later. She offers her ring as collateral, but the hotel manager refuses it, telling her, "That won't be necessary. Mrs. Turner, I'd be honored, really."

Ike and Tina meet again in divorce court in 1977, where she tells the judge that she doesn't want alimony or royalties off their records. All she wants to keep is her stage name, "Tina Turner." Ike even protests granting this — but that plea falls on deaf ears. The judge agrees, and now Tina's completely on her own.

Tina continues to tour and entertain, but still Ike isn't out of her life. He tracks her down in a parking lot and tries to get her to come back to him. But she won't be taken in again. Later, their oldest son shows up at her house, beaten up by Ike. He tells her that Ike has been brandishing a gun and saying that he would get her.

Still, Tina is a determined woman. At age 43, she's trying to make a major comeback. In her dressing room before her big debut, Ike shows up with that gun, but she walks away from him and out on stage where she performs the film's closing number, the title song, "What's Love Got to Do With It?" Before the song is complete, Angela Bassett has metamorphosed into the real Tina Turner performing this song, which became a number one hit.

The script-on-scene notes that Ike later served time in a California prison on drug charges and that Tina's first solo album won four Grammy Awards, including Record of the Year.

What's Love Got to Do With It? is a powerful and disturbing motion picture, filled with fine acting all around, especially by the two major stars. Although the songs we hear are sung by Tina, you would hardly know it; so precise is Angela Bassett's synchronization to Tina's style, you could almost believe she was Tina. And Laurence Fishburne is truly frightening as Ike Turner.

Even though the scenes in St. Louis are brief, this is a story that would not have existed without it.

Kevin Kline
Born October 24, 1947

Versatility is the key word to use when describing the acting ability of Kevin Kline. The St. Louis native has been well received for his work in classical drama, in zany comedy, and in musical theater.

Born in 1947, Kevin began acting while he was growing up, performing in various school plays while a student at the St. Louis Priory School. He left his hometown after high school to attend Indiana University, where he concentrated on composing and conducting music his first two years, before deciding to concentrate on drama. It was while a student at Indiana that he co-founded The Vest Pocket Players, a troupe that performed satirical skits.

After graduation from Indiana, Kevin went on to study at the Juilliard School in New York City. When he was 25, he began working in John Houseman's Acting Company, where he toured, performing the works of William Shakespeare.

For his subsequent work in musical theater, he received two Tony Awards, for his performances in *The Pirates of Penzance* and *On the Twentieth Century*. Then, for a while, he played the character Woody Reed on the long-running daytime soap opera, *Search for Tomorrow*.

Kevin's first motion picture appearance was in 1982's *Sophie's Choice*, and he was nominated for a Golden Globe Award for his portrayal of the character Nathan Landau.

After *Sophie*, the film roles have come regularly for Kevin Kline. Between 1983 and 1989, he appeared in seven productions: *The Pirates of Penzance*; *The Big Chill*; *Silverado*; *Violets Are Blue*; *Cry Freedom*; *A Fish Called Wanda* (for which he received an Oscar in the Best Supporting Actor category); and *January Man*.

In the 1990s, Kevin appeared in 13 films: *I Love You to Death*; *Soapdish*; *Grand Canyon*; *Consenting Adults*; *Chaplin*; *Dave*; *Princess Caraboo*; *French*

Kevin Kline in the movie *Dave*

Kiss; Fierce Creatures; The Ice Storm; In & Out; A Midsummer Night's Dream; and *The Wild Wild West.* In addition, he was in a 1990 television version of *Hamlet,* and he lent his voice to three productions: *Merlin and the Dragons, The Nutcracker,* and *The Hunchback of Notre Dame.*

In the first half of the post-2000 decade, he has already made seven motion pictures: *The Road to El Dorado* (voice); *The Anniversary Party; Life As a House; Orange County; The Hunchback of Notre Dame II* (voice); *The Emperor's Club;* and *De-Lovely.*

Kevin's versatility is evident in an examination of some his other roles, everything from the dimwit Otto in *A Fish Called Wanda* (which won him an Academy Award) to Douglas Fairbanks in *Chaplin,* and from playing Hamlet in *Hamlet* to Howard Brackett, a sexually conflicted teacher in *In & Out.*

And he has, to date, played the President of the United States in two different productions, the fictitious Bill Mitchell in *Dave* and the very real Ulysses Grant, albeit in a fictional setting, in *The Wild Wild West,* a movie in which he also played one of the lead characters, Artemus Gordon.

Kevin Kline has been called "a real theatrical actor," similar in style to thespians of old, who often had to change roles several times in an evening filled with short and varied performances designed to reach a wide audience.

King of the Hill
1993

Directed by Steven Soderbergh
Written by A.E. Hotchner (book)
and Steven Soderbergh (screenplay)

Primary Cast:

Aaron Kurlander	*Jesse Bradford*
Erich Kurlander	*Jeroen Krabbe*
Mrs. Kurlander	*Lisa Eichhorn*
Miss Mathey	*Karen Allen*
Mr. Mungo	*Spalding Gray*
Lydia	*Elizabeth McGovern*
Sullivan Kurlander	*Cameron Boyd*
Lester Silverstone	*Adrien Brody*
Hotel Porter	*Joe Chrest*
"Big Butt" Burns	*John McConnell*
Ella McShane	*Amber Benson*
Mrs. McShane	*Kristin Griffith*
Billy Thompson	*Chris Samples*
Mrs. Thompson	*Peggy Freisen*
Christina Sebastian	*Katherine Heigl*
Mr. Sandoz	*John Durbin*
Elevator Operator	*Lauryn Hill*

KING OF THE HILL

When
the world
turns
upside down
the trick is
coming out
on top.

GRAMERCY PICTURES PRESENTS A WILDWOOD/BONA FIDE PRODUCTION
"KING OF THE HILL" JEROEN KRABBÉ LISA EICHHORN KAREN ALLEN SPALDING GRAY
ELIZABETH MCGOVERN AND JESSE BRADFORD AS AARON COSTUME DESIGN SUSAN LYALL PRODUCTION DESIGN GARY FRUTKOFF
MUSIC CLIFF MARTINEZ CAMERA ELLIOT DAVIS BASED ON THE MEMOIR BY A.E. HOTCHNER EXECUTIVE PRODUCER JOHN HARDY
PRODUCED BY BARBARA MALTBY ALBERT BERGER RON YERXA
STEREO SURROUND PG-13 WRITTEN FOR THE SCREEN AND DIRECTED BY STEVEN SODERBERGH

ON VIDEOCASSETTE
Also Available On Laserdisc

GRAMERCY
PICTURES

Principal Stillwater	*Remak Ramsay*
Pet Store Owner	*Don Richard*

Steven Soderbergh came to the Gateway City in the early 1990s to find the yesteryear of A.E. Hotchner's memoir, *King of the Hill.* It was here and right across the Mississippi River in Alton that he filmed this story, set in Depression-era St. Louis, a tale filled with despair and hope and determination — the story of a 12-year-old boy surviving on his own by his quick wits.

Aaron Kurlander (played by Jesse Bradford) has a vivid imagination. We see that in the film's opening scene, in which he's reading (to his classmates) a story he's written, a concoction about how his friend, Charles A. Lindbergh, often calls to ask his advice.

It's 1933, and St. Louis, like the rest of the country, is filled with people scrambling just to stay alive. The Great Depression is in full swing, and Aaron's family members are some of its victims. His father (Jeroen Krabbe) is a proud man determined to find work, a man who somehow remains optimistic that he *will* get one of two jobs, either selling Hamilton Watches or working for President Roosevelt's WPA. But, for the time being, he's holed up in a hotel with his wife (Lisa Eichhorn) and his two sons.

Those sons, though several years apart in age, are quite close, and, as the older brother, Aaron is constantly looking out for Sullivan (Cameron Boyd). He shows Sullivan how to play marbles, races through the neighborhood with the younger boy, and warns Sullivan to never reveal to his classmates or teachers that his family is living in a hotel. Like his father, Aaron is very proud, and he doesn't want others to know about his family's destitute situation. So he puts up a front at school, where many of his classmates are children of the wealthy.

As they are returning from school, we see the brothers play their way through the streets. Then, when they arrive "home" at the Empire Hotel, we briefly meet such characters as Arletta (Lauryn Hill), the elevator operator, and Ben (Joe Chrest), the hotel porter who is busy locking out one of the boys' neighbors, Mr. Sandoz (John Durbin), an artist who has painted a portrait of Aaron, because of non-payment of rent. We see the two men fighting when the neighbor tries to get inside the locked room. Rushing in on their parents after watching the battle in the hallway, the two boys find an unusually somber atmosphere in their own room. "Did somebody die?" Aaron asks immediately. No, no one has died, but it's something like a death for Aaron. His parents have decided to send Sullivan away to live with an uncle in Iowa. Aaron protests the decision, but to no avail. Before his brother rides away in the picturesque, antique Greyhound Bus, Aaron gives Sullivan his best marble.

It soon becomes obvious that Aaron's mother isn't well. Her eyes are sunken, and she has a deep cough. Soon, she, too, is gone from Aaron's day-to-day life. His father takes her to the sanitarium, where she must stay for some months to recover from what people used to call "consumption."

At school, Aaron makes friends with one of the rich kids in his class, Billy Thompson, by coming to his aid when two older boys are trying to force Billy to shoot marbles with them. Aaron is an expert marksman and wipes out the two other boys. Afterward, Billy invites Aaron over after school. In Billy's family mansion, Aaron finds himself making up tales about his father in order to avoid revealing his family's destitute situation. Billy sends Aaron home with the gift of a female canary to breed with the male he already has, so he can raise young canaries, like Billy, and sell them for $3 each to Mr. Farley, the local pet store owner.

We meet Aaron's "older" friend, Lester Silverstone (played by a very young Adrien Brody), a teenager who has a shady side, but is very likeable, and who seems to have a great affection for the younger boy. We also meet Aaron's teacher, Miss Mathey (Karen Allen), who tells Aaron that the school needs a correct address for him so she can be sure he's in the correct district to attend her school. When he makes up another whopper, it's obvious that she realizes his story is fictitious, but even after she follows him and discovers he lives in a hotel, she never reveals his secret.

Others in Aaron's life include the annoying traffic cop, "Big Butt" Burns (John McConnell), who likes to grab boys by their ears and threaten them; and another of his neighbors, Mr. Mungo (played in a marvelously low-key manner by Spalding Gray), a man who used to be rich before the stock-market crash, but who now finds himself living marginally in a room in the Empire Hotel across the hall from Aaron and consorting with prostitutes. There's also Ella McShane (Amber Benson), another of Aaron's neighbors, a girl probably a year or so older but who obviously has a crush on the boy. While he's dancing with her in her room one afternoon, she collapses with an epileptic seizure, frightening Aaron, until the girl's mother comes to her rescue.

With his brother and mother gone, there's only Aaron and his father in the room now, and Aaron makes what his father calls "tasty" ketchup soup for the two of them — but not for long. One day, "Big Butt" Burns grabs him by the ear and tricks him into revealing where his father has hidden his car. As soon as he does, Aaron realizes that "Big Butt" will give the information to his "repo" buddies. So he informs Lester what he's done, and the two of them rush over to the car, and, with Aaron behind the wheel, Lester pushes the out-of-gas vehicle down a hill. Aaron can steer the vehicle quite well, it seems, but he can't reach the peddles, so he goes careening downward (in a scene obviously shot in the bluffside area of Alton), basically out of control, in one of the most exciting portions in the film. Finally, he starts up a hill and begins to roll backward but is able to steer the car into the curb and stop it. When he arrives home, he finds his father packing. He's been offered the job with Hamilton watches, and his territory is out of state, so now he tells the boy he must leave him to fend for himself. He does say that he has given one of his expensive sample watches to a waiter, who will provide his son with food, and another to the hotel to cover part of the overdue rent.

So now Aaron is all alone in the hotel room.

When he goes to the restaurant to eat, he finds that the owner has found out about the waiter's "arrangements" and fired the man, so now Aaron has no food except for 20 dinner rolls, which he buys for a quarter at the restaurant, and he eats these slowly over the next several days.

The boy's efforts to raise money aren't very successful, it seems. His canaries are now old enough to take to the pet store, but when they're checked, the owner asserts that all of the young birds are female (which do not sing), so all four of his birds bring only 50 cents instead of the $12 he had been expecting. He uses the money to buy a kitten for Ella, who has had another seizure and is now bedridden. Her mother says that they, too, will be leaving soon to go live with her sister in Illinois.

At school, Aaron sneaks food from some of the rich kids to supplement his steady diet of dinner rolls. He and his classmates are preparing for graduation from grammar school, and one of the girls asks Aaron if he would join her and her family for a special dinner after the graduation reception at Billy Thompson's house.

When he arrives "home" from school one day, Aaron finds a letter to his father from the WPA, so he addresses an envelope to the man in care of the Hamilton Watch Company in Pennsylvania and stuffs the WPA letter inside.

Preparing for his graduation ceremony, Aaron discovers that he has outgrown his only suit, but his friend Lester comes to his rescue. The two of them break into the room full of confiscated belongings at the hotel and find a suit for Aaron to wear. Then, at the ceremony, Aaron is alone except for Lester standing at the back of the room cheering for him when he is chosen as the one member of his class to receive an Achievement Award, for demonstrating both "scholastic achievement" and "good character." However, after graduation, at the reception, other members of his class begin to make fun of Aaron because they've discovered discrepancies in the wild tales he's told about his family, and also because some have figured out that he's a poor kid. So he runs into the bathroom and climbs out the window, fleeing Billy's home and leaving his diploma and his special award behind.

Back at the hotel, things have begun to fall apart, too. He finds that the management has given him three days to pay the $172 back rent (a tremendous sum in the 1930s), or he will be locked out of his room. He's also missing his little brother so much that he forges his father's name on a note to his uncle, asking him to send Sullivan back to St. Louis. While he's resting in his room, he hears a lot of noise and goes outside to discover the police destroying a tent city in which the homeless had been living. He also sees his friend Lester being dragged away by the police.

Going back into the hotel, he discovers that the porter has decided to go ahead and lock him out even though the three days aren't expired. However, Aaron runs past him and locks the door. He holes up inside without food for days, enduring the constant banging by the porter. He only comes out when he sees water running out of Mr. Mungo's room across the hall. When he enters, he discovers that his friend has slit his wrists and is dead. Aaron rushes back into his own room and vigorously washes the blood from his hands. Inside the room, eventually, he begins to cramp and goes into a delirious state, in which he sees distorted visions. He only comes out when he hears a gentle tapping at the door, very different from the porter's. When he opens it, there stands his brother. And Sullivan has food with him.

The two brothers sit at the table eating and enjoying each other's company. Afterward, while playing marbles, they hear another sound at the door. Their father has also arrived. It seems he's been offered the WPA job, thanks to Aaron's forwarding the letter to him. Now he's going to get their mother and move the family to a nice apartment. But the two boys refuse to leave the hotel without their belongings, so the father goes ahead to get their mother, while Aaron and Sullivan smuggle their possessions out a window on a makeshift rope made of sheets.

The movie's conclusion is basically low key: At the apartment complex, it's a bittersweet reunion for Aaron with his family, especially his father, whom he obviously resents for abandoning him to fend for himself. But, at least they are all together again in a nice place.

King of the Hill is a very touching film about family, love, and coming of age under very difficult circumstances, and it's filled with an abundance of nicely developed characters of all varieties.

Those who look closely will recognize a number of the St. Louis and Alton locations and should find this to be another rewarding film about the old hometown.

Parts of the film were shot in The Central West End at Taylor and Olive Boulevards (courtesy of *West End Word*)

John Goodman
Born June 20, 1952

John Goodman is a major film and television star who has great affection for his hometown. Born in the St. Louis suburb of Affton, he still has strong ties to the land of his birth.

"I don't think there's a finer place on Earth than St. Louis, Missouri. It works for me. I'm very comfortable in St. Louis. The people are great, and, if I have my way, I'll live there again some day," he notes in his Foreword to this book.

It's in the Big Apple or in Hollywood where many famous actors say they got that "big break" that spurred them on to stardom, but John Goodman contends that never happened to him. "I never had a big break. I had a series of unfortunate little breaks. It boiled down to being able to provide for myself with commercials. In acting school, they were always looked down on and pooh-poohed, but when that bread came in, it was great. I could pick and chose roles, and I didn't have to go on the road with dinner theater fare all the time. I could stay in New York and work."

Actually, John's first appearance on television was in a Burger King commercial in which he didn't speak, but just ate a Whopper. However, there is that TV role a few years later for which many fondly remember him, the role of Dan Conner, the husband and father on the long-running series, *Roseanne*.

"I had a pretty good film career going before I started doing the *Roseanne* TV series," he relates in his Foreword. "But one of the reasons I took *Roseanne* was that I was tired of living out of a suitcase, going from movie to movie."

Prior to 1988, the year that he was cast in *Roseanne*, John had already appeared in 11 theatrical films and four television productions: *Jailbait Baby*; *The Face of Rage*; *Eddie Macon's Run*; *The Survivors*; *Chiefs* (TV mini-series); *Heart of Steel*; *Revenge of the Nerds*; *C.H.U.D.*; *Maria's Lovers*; *Sweet Dreams*;

John Goodman in *The Borrowers*

True Stories; Raising Arizona; Burglar; The Big Easy; and *Murder Ordained.*

From 1988 through 1997, the years that *Roseanne* was on the air, he actually made 22 theatrical and television movies: *The Wrong Guys; Punchline; Everybody's All-American; Sea of Love; Always; Stella; Arachnophobia; King Ralph; Barton Fink* (for which he received a Golden Globe nomination for Best Supporting Actor); *The Babe; Frosty Returns* (voice); *Matinee; Born Yesterday; We're Back! A Dinosaur's Story* (voice); *The Hudsucker Proxy; The Flintstones; Kingfish: A Story of Huey P. Long; A Streetcar Named Desire; Pyst; Pie in the Sky; Mother Night;* and *The Borrowers.*

During the last two years of the 1990s, he did another 11 productions: *Fallen; Blues Brothers 2000; The Big Lebowski; Dirty Work; The Real Macaw* (voice); *Rudolph the Red-Nosed Reindeer: The Movie* (voice); *The Runner; Saturday Night Live: Best of the Clinton Scandal; The Jack Bull; Now and Again* (TV series); and *Bringing Out the Dead.*

Ever the performing workhorse, John has been featured in 25 projects since the year 2000: *What Planet Are You From?; O Brother Where Art Thou?; The Adventures of Rocky & Bullwinkle; Coyote Ugly; Pigs Next Door* (voice); *Normal, Ohio* (TV series); *The Emperor's New Groove* (voice); *My First Mister; One Night at McCool's, Storytelling, On the Edge* (TV series), *Happy Birthday, Monsters Inc.* (voice); *Mike's New Car* (voice); *Dirty Deeds; Masked and Anonymous; The Jungle Book 2* (voice); *Home of Phobia; Clifford's Really Big Movie* (voice); *Father of the Pride* (voice; TV series); *Center of the Universe* (TV series); *Beyond the Sea; Marilyn Hotchkiss' Ballroom Dancing and Charm School; Kronk's New Groove;* and *Drunkboat.*

At the beginning of the 2004-05 season, he literally had two TV shows debuting, but neither made it far beyond the starting gate and were cancelled before the year was over. "They were both very expensive," he recalls. "The cartoon show (*Father of the Pride*) was really ridiculously expensive. It was slanted more toward adults, and when they do that, it usually gets pretty gratuitous. But the stuff with Siegfried and Roy was funnier than hell to me. Still, with a cartoon like that, kids are going to watch, and some of the sexual stuff was a little uncomfortable to do just because I knew there were going to be a lot of kids watching. Then with the other series (*Center of the Universe*), they cast too many [big] names in it, and they had to pay everybody, so they didn't leave much money for the writing. And the network just hated it from jump street, anyway; they never promoted it. But it was fun. It's always fun to work on something like that because it's like a family situation. You come every day and try to solve problems, and you hang out. Yet I just knew it was doomed, so I tried to have as much fun as I could."

With the strong feelings that John Goodman has for St. Louis, he's hopeful of some day soon coming back to his hometown to appear on the legitimate stage, something that he continues to love. But it will need to be the right project at the right time, obviously, to fit into his very busy schedule. "I reckon I'm a real hometown St. Louisan," he asserts in his Foreword.

John Goodman in *King Ralph*

The Big Brass Ring
1999

Directed by George Hickenlooper

Written by Orson Welles and Oja Kodar (original script);

F.X. Feeney and George Hickenlooper (screenplay)

Primary Cast:

William Blake Pellarin	*William Hurt*
Dinah Pellarin	*Miranda Richardson*
Kim Mennaker	*Nigel Hawthorne*
Cela Brandini	*Irene Jacob*
Kinzel	*Ewan Stewart*
Billy	*Gregg Henry*
Sheldon Buckle	*Ron Livingston*
Garne Strickland	*Jefferson Mays*
Packy Barragan	*Jim Metzler*
Young Billy	*Carmine Giovinazzo*
Young Blake	*Thomas Patrick Kelly*
Homer Dix	*Mack Harrell*
B.C. Dix	*Lisette Bross*
Senator Jack Moorehead	*F. Joseph Schulte*
Gigi Moorehead	*Peggy Freisen*

Orson Welles began his motion picture career with a film that he wrote and directed, a film that some have called "the greatest movie of all

William Hurt as William Blake Pellarin

times" — *Citizen Kane*. When he wrote the original script for *The Big Brass Ring*, some say that this was to be the other half of the "bookends" that began with that other great production, but he never lived to see this story put on celluloid.

Primarily set in (and filmed in) St. Louis, *The Big Brass Ring* is a dark and convoluted tale of a candidate for governor of Missouri whom many believe will one day be President of the United States.

In a major twist on the traditional American two-party political system, Blake Pellarin (William Hurt) is an independent candidate whose primary opponent for the job, Homer Dix (Mack Harrell), is also an independent, but with a different philosophical bent.

The film opens with a quote from Abraham Lincoln: "It is common enough that we triumph under adversity, but if you truly wish to test a man's character, give him power." But the sexual scene to which that comment is the backdrop doesn't quite fit — at that moment. Later on in the story, we understand the significance of that display.

Cut to the credits and a scene with Blake Pellarin giving a speech before some of his supporters. His wife, Dinah (Miranda Richardson), comes rushing in late, but she stands offstage with some of Pellarin's associates, smoking a cigarette.

We see a black and white scene with two young boys playing together in a classic Cadillac convertible, and, later on, we realize that these scenes at the very opening are flashbacks, something that occurs throughout this production.

Next, we see a newscast from a national cable news and entertainment channel on which the main character is introduced in a news report by primary character, Cela Brandini (Irene Jacob). The broadcast account is about how two independent candidates for governor in Missouri are the leading contenders for the job, possibly spelling the beginning of the end for the two-party political system in this country.

The opening six minutes of the film take place in the western edge of the state (in and around Kansas City); then Pellarin flies into St. Louis, where the rest of the story transpires. We see lots of scenes of the Arch and the riverfront, as well as numerous familiar streets and buildings, all located in the downtown area.

After a brief crowd scene with Pellarin walking on Laclede's Landing, there is another newscast by Cela in which she interviews former maverick U.S. Senator Kim Mennaker, who has been living for a number years somewhat in exile in Cuba. The connection to the main part of the story comes into focus when she reveals that the ex-senator from Rhode Island in fact became a surrogate parent to Blake Pellarin after the death of both of his parents. We can also see that this is an older version of the man photographing the sex scene at the beginning of the film.

Now we see more flashbacks, in detail, from that sexual photo shoot, and we see a young white man and a young black man together in a homosexual encounter.

Back to the present, with more panoramic scenes from the city, and it's revealed that the election is only four days away. This is followed by a scene with a man in a wheelchair living in poverty with a monkey (literally) on his back, as he watches a television showing Pellarin campaigning. As the man is sitting in front of the TV, Mennaker comes in and offers crutches to the man in the wheelchair. On a table behind the man is a framed photograph of the two young boys we saw earlier, playing in the old Cadillac.

Blake Pellarin is holding an impromptu news conference while eating an ice cream on the steps of Arch, and, as he gets up to leave, he is approached by Cela Brandini, who asks him: "Who is Raymond Romero?" But he chooses not to answer and walks away from her.

Later, Pellarin is standing, staring out across the Mississippi, and obviously remembering. There is another flashback scene with two young men, one in military uniform preparing to board a train. The two, who look a great deal alike, are arguing. A homeless man asking for a handout brings Blake back to the present. Later, in a car with his aides, Pellarin is being dressed down by one of these assistants, who also asks: "Who is Raymond Romero?" And Pellarin declares it's a trick by Mennaker. In the next scene, the aide (Jefferson Mays) is fired by Dinah Pellarin, who tells him that it's "this time for keeps."

Pellarin finds an envelope with the name "Raymond Romero" printed on it while he's aboard the riverboat that is his St. Louis campaign headquarters. And in that envelope is a photo of the two young men who engaged in the homosexual photo shoot in the flashback. With the photo, there is also a matchbook reading: "The Louis Quatorze."

Everything that has occurred in this story to this point is enigmatic, but the elements soon start to sort themselves out.

At a black-tie, political get-together, where both of the two major parties are courting the two independents to join them, we first meet the other candidate, Homer Dix, who bills himself as a "good ol' boy" that is known to the voters, in contrast to Pellarin, whom he says is an unknown factor. At this same affair, Pellarin is cornered in, of all places, the men's room, by the reporter who stopped him on the Arch steps, and she's still inquiring about the identity of Raymond Romero. Nevertheless, Pellarin gives her no answers.

But we begin to get answers shortly afterward when Pellarin shows the photo to his wife, who says the young man in the homosexual photo looks a lot like Blake. But he says it isn't — that it's his brother, Raymond. Dinah burns the photo, but we know that the situation won't be that easily resolved.

Bit by bit, over the next several scenes and through flashbacks and discussions, the truth begins to come out. Pellarin seeks out Brandini in her mobile television van, where's she's editing material, and he tells her that Raymond was his brother, that they had different last names because they were born out of wedlock, and that his brother is dead. She persists and wants to know how Raymond died, but the candidate reserves this piece of information.

Later, Pellarin, who has learned that the "Louis Quatorze" is a showboat for homosexual men, travels alone by a small racing boat and boards the "Louis Quatorze," where he finds the old dissident, Kim Mennaker. There, we learn more of the answers to the mystery. It seems that Pellarin isn't Pellarin at all. He is actually Raymond Romero, himself. The two brothers came of age during the Vietnam War era, and when Raymond's number came up in the draft, his brother, Billy, took his identity and went off to fight in his place. There is an insinuation that Mennaker wanted it this way, so he could keep Raymond with him, since Raymond was always his favorite. "The name William Blake was wasted on him," the ex-senator declares to the young Raymond in one of the flashback scenes.

So Billy — the real William Blake Pellarin — went off to fight in that war in Southeast Asia three decades earlier, and he died there. That is what Blake Pellarin — the real Raymond Romero — has believed for more than half his life, and he resented his brother for what he did, along with "the old man." But now Mennaker has some more news for Pellarin: Billy isn't dead after all, he says. He was badly injured — maimed — in Vietnam, but he isn't dead. He's been living in Cuba.

Mennaker further reveals what hasn't been a well-kept secret. He has been grooming Pellarin since he was a youth to one day become President, but he could never have had a chance if his name were Romero. The electorate wouldn't pick a man with a Hispanic surname. Now, he feels that Pellarin is about to take the long-anticipated first step before achieving that goal, and he wants Blake to resurrect him when he does reach the White House and make him Secretary of State. Pellarin refuses, even when Mennaker threatens to expose him, and he walks out.

The former Rhode Island senator makes good on his threat and sends one of the photos to Pellarin's opponent, Homer Dix, who, of course, is prepared to expose Pellarin. But Blakes acts before Dix. He goes to see the other man with a photo of his own, which shows a man who looks like a younger Dix, a man dressed in Ku Klux Klan garments at a Klan rally, a man with "KKK" tattooed on his fingers, the same fingers that are now scarred on Dix's hand.

But the intrigue isn't over yet. It seems that Dinah Pellarin has decided to dismiss Kinzel (Ewan Stewart), the chauffer and security guard, whom she feels has heard too much; but the man tells her that he won't just go away. No, she'll have to pay him off, he says. So she agrees.

Pellarin picks up the money for Kinzel and brings it to a restaurant, where he meets his wife. While they're there, the reporter, Brandini, shows up. But Pellarin gets into a confrontation with Dinah, and she walks out. When Pellarin goes after her, Brandini says she'll take care of his briefcase. When he returns to the restaurant, she is gone, also, but she has left word where Pellarin can find her. When he goes to her loft, she hugs him and kisses him, and they end up spending the night together.

Afterward, when Pellarin calls on Mennaker again, the former senator tells him that his brother is now in St. Louis. Pellarin goes to find Billy and takes the money along to give to him instead of Kinzel. The two brothers are overjoyed to be together again and hug each other. But Kinzel comes for his money, and when he finds Mennaker outside the hotel where Billy is staying, he kills the old man. Then he bursts in on the two brothers. When he pulls a gun, Pellarin knocks Billy to the floor and covers him with his body. After threatening to kill them both, Kinzel grabs the money and leaves.

You would think with all that has happened, the truth would come out, and Pellarin's political career would be over. But not so in this film. Mennaker's death is reported by the media as being caused by a cerebral hemorrhage, and Pellarin goes on to beat Homer Dix by seven percentage points. "Democratic and Republican leaders in all corners of the country are nervous tonight — pondering, as one pundit put it, the meaning of Blake Pellarin," the voice-over newscaster says, as the governor-elect celebrates at Union Station.

The film ends with Billy — the Billy of today — pulling himself along on crutches on the edge of St. Louis' Mississippi riverfront.

Several local faces familiar to St. Louisans appear in cameo roles as themselves in "newscasts" in this production. Among those featured are Dick Ford and Mandy Murphey (Fox 2), Cree Craig and Brenda Stanton (WB 11), and Leslie Lyles (ABC 30) — all reporting on the fictional campaign for governor.

The Big Brass Ring is, indeed, dark and foreboding throughout, and William Hurt certainly plays his character-with-a-secret well. But this is definitely a depressing film. Like Welles' earlier *Citizen Kane*, this story deals with the disturbing aspects of political life. Still, this is no *Citizen Kane*; make no doubt about that. When one paints a masterpiece first, it's difficult to create an encore. Still and all, *The Big Brass Ring* isn't a bad film. A bit slow and plodding, but it's a worthy effort. If you don't mind the depressing aspects (which is most of the production), you may appreciate Welles' last hurrah.

And, for St. Louisans, there is a lot to see of the old home town....

Scott Bakula

Born October 9, 1954

Science fiction fans are familiar with Scott Bakula as a man who has spent a lot of time traveling around space or back in time. But he's had time during the last two decades to appear in more than a dozen feature films, as well as many television productions.

Variously know to his loyal sci-fi followers as Captain Jonathan Archer in *Star Trek: Enterprise* and as Dr. Sam Beckett in *Quantum Leap*, Scott was born in St. Louis.

Scott Bakula began his career as an entertainer with his own band, which he put together when he was in the fourth grade. Then he went on to perform with the St. Louis Symphony when he was older. However, he had not planned on having a theatrical career. In fact, he studied law at the University of Kansas.

In 1986, Scott made his first appearance on television in the TV film, *I-Man*, followed by the starring role in the short-run sitcom *Gung Ho* (based on the movie of the same name), then in the *Matlock* TV movie, *The Power Brokers*, that same year. Other appearances followed in 1987, in the TV films *The Last Fling* and *Infiltrator*; and, in 1988, he starred in another short-run sitcom, *Eisenhower and Lutz*.

Then, his big break came in 1989, when he was cast in the lead on *Quantum Leap*, a series that lasted until 1993. After his face became familiar across the land, it was much easier for Scott to get major roles. He appeared in the theatrical films *Sibling Rivalry* in 1990 and *Necessary Roughness* in 1991. The next year, he played a detective in the TV movie, *In the Shadow of a Killer*, and was in the theatrical film, *For Goodness Sake*, in 1993 and another TV film, *Mercy Mission: The Rescue of Flight 771*, that same year.

Post-*Quantum Leap* films included *A Passion to Kill* and *Color of Night* and the TV movie, *Nowhere to Hide*, all in 1994, and *My Family, Lord of*

Scott Bakula attended Kirkwood High School, class of 1973
(courtesy Dan Dillon)

Illusions, plus the TV film, *The Invaders*, in 1995.

In the latter half of the 1990s, Scott appeared in such TV films as *The Bachelor's Baby*, *NetForce*, and *Mean Streak*, as well as the theatrical films, *Major League: Back to the Minors* and *American Beauty*. He also starred in another short-lived TV series, *Mr. & Mrs. Smith*, about two CIA agents who pose as a married couple when on their gambits.

Some of his post-2000 films have included *Above Suspicion*, *Luminaries*, *Role of a Lifetime*, and *Life As a House*. TV productions have included *The Trial of Old Drum*, *In the Name of the People*, *Papa's Angels*, and *What Girls Learn*. In 2001, he boarded *Star Trek: Enterprise* for a grand tour of the galaxy.

Scott won a Golden Globe Award in 1992 for his role of Sam Beckett in *Quantum Leap*, and he previously had been nominated for a Tony Award for work on Broadway in *Romance/Romance*. He is the only actor to be listed in two different roles in *TV Guide* magazine's "Legends of Sci-Fi."

Scott keeps in shape by running. He completed the 2005 Los Angeles Marathon in just over four hours and ten minutes.

The Game of Their Lives
2005

Directed by David Anspaugh
Written by Geoffrey Douglas & Angelo Pizzo

Primary Cast:

Frank Borghi	*Gerard Butler*
Walter Bahr	*Wes Bentley*
Joe Maca	*Richard Jenik*
Frank "Pee Wee" Wallace	*Jay Rodan*
Virgininio "Gino" Pariani	*Louis Mandylor*
Charlie "Gloves" Columbo	*Costas Mandylor*
Joe Gatjaens	*Jimmy Jean-Louis*
Harry Keough	*Zachery Bryan*
John "Clarkie" Souza	*Nelson Vargas*
Dent McSkimming (older)	*Patrick Stewart*
Dent McSkimming (younger)	*Terry Kinney*
Bill Jeffrey	*John Rhys-Davis*
Stanley Mortenson	*Gavin Rossdale*
Rosemary Borghi	*Maria Bertrand*
Janet Capiello	*Julie Granata*
Ed McIlvenny	*John Harkes*
Walter Giesler	*Craig Hawksley*
General Higgins	*Bill Smitrovich*

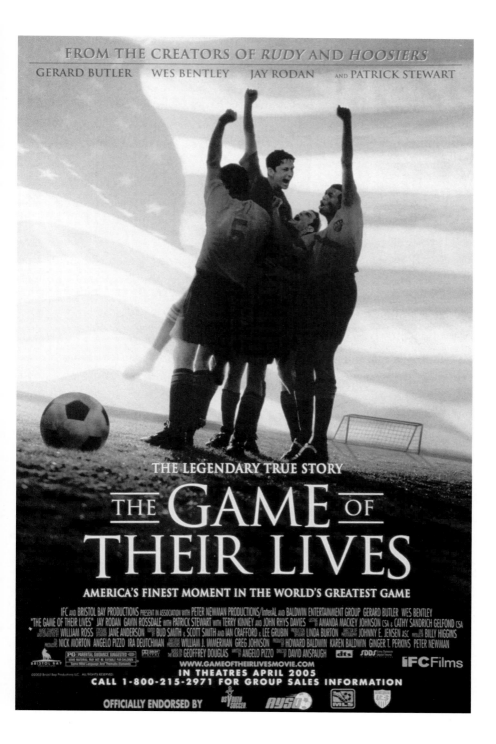

Soccer never has become a "hot" sport in this country, but, in 1950, for a group of guys from St. Louis' mostly Italian neighborhood known as "The Hill," it was their ticket to sports immortality.

The Game of the Lives is the true story of how Team USA — with several of its best players from St. Louis — took on the best soccer team in world, the English, and beat them in the World Cup matches in a small town in Brazil.

The film opens with a present-day soccer match in progress. In the stands is retired *Post-Dispatch* reporter Dent McSkimming (Patrick Stewart), who is approached by a young man who asks McSkimming to tell him the story of the 1950 American soccer team.

That's when the flashback begins. Stewart's character explains that although baseball was popular with second and third-generation Italian Americans on The Hill — after all, he points out, both Yogi Berra and Joe Garagiola came from that part of St. Louis — soccer was the sporting passion of young men who lived there.

"Like many immigrant communities all over America, The Hill had one foot in the old country and one in the new," McSkimming explained. "An area of about 20 square blocks, The Hill was a tightly knit, self-contained enclave."

This is where we meet the main characters. There's the soccer team's goalie, Frank (Gerard Butler), plus players Walter (Wes Bentley), Gino (Louis Mandylor), Joe (Richard Jenik), Gloves (Costas Mandylor), and the younger *Post-Dispatch* reporter Dent McSkimming (Terry Kinney). But, as Stewart's character (who narrates the entire film) explains, covering the soccer matches wasn't just a job for Dent; it was a passion, much like playing soccer was for the other guys.

These players form a closely knit amateur team, and the players are friends who also hang out together when they're not on the soccer field. But when they're playing the game they love, they're serious about it. They play to win, and they *do*, most of the time.

Then something striking happens in their tiny soccer world. That's when the guys are informed that a New York team is coming to play against them, and that from that group, individuals would be chosen to constitute the United States official team that would compete in the World Cup in

Brazil. These friends are excited, but they're confident. Several express the belief that they are certain to make the national team. But one notable player, Gino, declares that he cannot become a member of the big team even if he is chosen, because his wedding is set for when the team would be in Brazil. His teammates and their manager (Craig Hawksley) try to convince him that he should reschedule his wedding; but he contends that such is impossible because everything is already set up and even the invitations have been sent out.

Gino's problem is quickly solved, however, when the manager contacts Gino's prospective father-in-law and tells him that the team really needs Gino. That's when Gino is informed by the older man that the solution is simple. The wedding will simply be moved up, not back, and he'll get married before he leaves. Since he's already contacted the church and reception hall and rescheduled them, all that's left is for Gino to do is personally deliver the new invitations.

Then there's Frank (Gerard Butler), whose family owns a funeral parlor; when he asks off for three weeks to take part in the soccer event, should he be chosen, his mother refuses, telling him that embalming school starts in two weeks. That's when he declares that he does not plan to be an undertaker. His wife, Rosemary (Maria Bertrand), tries to console him, but he declares that he will go to New York and Brazil if he is chosen.

Finally, there's Pee Wee, a decorated World War II veteran (like many of the others), who says he can't go because of his fear of flying. Of course, his friends hassle him over this, but they assure him that they'll get him drunk or whatever it takes to get him on the plane.

These all sound like conflicts for the major players. But they are resolved quickly in the story — actually much too quickly to keep the tension in the storyline. As it works out, all these guys are chosen for the national team after they play the New York team that comes to St. Louis to compete against them. Altogether, five St. Louisans make the team: Frank, Harry, Gloves, Pee Wee, and Gino.

Soon, these five St. Louisans head out by train for New York. Once in the Big Apple, the guys seem to be a little independent and reserved about blending in with the other players. Not only do they not immediately want to associate with the others off the field, but they seem to have a different style of play while on the field.

Then they're faced with their biggest challenge as a new group. The newly created American national team has only 10 days to practice together before they start competing internationally. Their first practice game, against a semi-pro team, shows how poorly the group of players works together. That's when some of the team leaders — namely team captain Walter Bahr (Wes Bentley) and Frank — decide to recruit a black East Indian, Joe Gatjaens (Jimmy Jean-Louis). They are discouraged by the coach, but they go out and locate Joe working in a restaurant kitchen and talk him into joining the team, anyway.

Constantly, the Americans keep asking their coach (played by distinguished British character actor John Rhys-Davis) when they will get their team uniforms, and he always says he's "working on it." But they never seem to materialize.

The American team slowly begins to mesh. That's when the coach announces that they will play a practice game against "a crack team" of British players, led by Stanley Mortenson (Gavin Rossdale), "arguably one of the greatest players in the past 50 years." When the game does take place, it demonstrates just how far they have to go to be able to compete against other major teams. The game, the second half of which is played in the pouring rain, proves to be a tremendous embarrassment to the Americans, with the British able to practically score at will.

After the game, Frank is so upset with his level of play that he refuses to ride back to the hotel on the bus. When the others try to coax him on, they find it futile, so several of his teammates climb off and walk back with him.

When the time comes to leave, Pee Wee is more than a little apprehensive, and, sure enough, his friends from St. Louis come up with something for him to drink that keeps him pacified for most of the flight. And it's a good thing, too, because the trip south is more than a little bumpy.

Finally, the team arrives in Rio de Janeiro, Brazil, and some see it as little more than a glorified holiday. When they read the odds, they discover that their team isn't even mentioned by the oddsmakers. So, some of the guys decide to go out on the town.

They are informed by the coach that their first game will be some 300 miles north of where they are in Rio, that they'll have to take another plane flight, and that when they arrive at Belo Horizonte, their first World Cup game will be against the very same British players who so recently humiliated them in New York.

However, as the team is preparing to leave for the game, they are met by a group of American military officials and, in a touching ceremony, each team member's name is called, along with mention of his accomplishments, as each man is presented with his new, official American World Cup soccer uniform by General Higgins (Bill Smitrovich).

Once in the stadium, the American players are overwhelmed at how large it is and by the fact that it's packed with eager soccer fans.

The actual game itself is played with a voiceover commentary by the English broadcasters beaming the game back to Great Britain. When the game gets underway, it's apparent that this is not the same team that lost terribly to these other guys just a few days before. No, they seem to have come together as a cohesive unit; and, very early in the game, the Americans score a goal. Surprisingly, it turns out to be the game's only goal. Frank, the American goalie, fights like a demon, warding off attempt after attempt by the British. In the end, he, along with his entire team, is exhausted, but they are happy, knowing that they've done the impossible. As a new, rank, and untested team, they have beaten the best soccer team in the world!

Afterward, with the flashback concluded, we see several members of that 1950s American World Cup team introduced to the crowd at the match that Dent McSkimming is attending and has been telling their story. As each is introduced, we see an image of the actor who played him as a young man in *The Game of Their Lives*.

There was some very strange casting in this film, with two very prominent British actors cast as Americans — Patrick Stewart (known to many for his portrayal of Jean-Luc Picard in the *Star Trek: The Next Generation* television series and films) and John Rhys-Davis (known for his many character roles, including playing Indiana Jones' Egyptian buddy in *Raiders of the Lost Ark*). In addition, the star of the British soccer team sounded suspiciously American. Go figure!

Although Stewart tries hard to affect an American accent, he strikes out in one very big way. Somebody should have informed him that people from St. Louis refer to themselves as "St. Louisans" and not "St. Louisians," as he says during his narrative of the story. Rhys-Davis is not terribly successful at being American, at all. No one would confuse his accent with that of a native-born son.

This film may leave some viewers disappointed, especially those who have come to see sports-event films with more dramatic tension. For those who are looking for a *Rocky* kind of ending, you won't find it here. Although this is definitely a story with character development, it has, nonetheless, something of a documentary feel about it.

Still, for St. Louisans — not St. Louisians — *The Game of Their Lives* should elicit a great deal of pride. Five guys from The Hill formed the core of an American team that made the nation proud. And, by the way, taking a peek at the way the city used to look a half-century ago isn't bad either.

Filming of *Game of their Lives* in St. Louis

CONCLUSION
The Gateway and Beyond

In this book I've told the stories of 14 films that have primarily St. Louis settings. But the story doesn't end with these movies. There are plenty more that "brush by" the Gateway City. And some were shot fully or partially in St. Louis, even though they aren't set in the city. Still other films feature the "outstate" area.

For instance, one of the films I devoted a chapter to is Steve Martin's *Parenthood*, a very fine production completely set in St. Louis without once mentioning the city by name. But there are a couple other Steve Martin films that touch on St. Louis, as well. His first major production, *The Jerk* (1979), sees Steve's character leaving the farm and working for a service station in St. Louis before heading out of town with the carnival. In *Planes, Trains & Automobiles* (1987), Steve's character is just trying to get home for Thanksgiving — stuck with an obnoxious fellow traveler, played by John Candy — and he's traveling by any means possible, attempting to reach his family. One of the filming locations was at St. Louis' Lambert Airport.

Films have been made in St. Louis for more than a century, it seems. The earliest I found was a one-minute silent newsreel, made in 1903, with a title almost as long as the film's running time: *President Roosevelt at the Dedication Ceremonies of the St. Louis Exposition*. Another film of note made in St. Louis during the silent era was a 1917 Civil War feature called *The Crisis* that was based on a novel written by a St. Louisan named Winston Churchill (not the British prime minister, of course).

Lots of other movies have been filmed completely or partially in the Gateway City over the decades. A few of these titles you might recognize: *Death on the Diamond* (1934); *Unusual Occupations* (1940); *Till it Helps!* (1959); *Number One* (1969); *The Crossroads Crash* (1973); *The World of Buckminster Fuller* (1974); *Stingray* (1978); *A Pleasure Doing Business* (1979); Cheech and Chong's *Things Are Tough All Over* (1982); *Highway 61* (1991); *Savage Harvest* (1994); *To Die, To Sleep* (1994); *Larger Than Life*, with Bill Murray (1996); *Angels of Mercy* (1997); *The Big One* (1997); *Ice From the Sun* (1999); *Scrapbook* (2000); *April Is My Religion* (2001); *Strawberry Spring*

(2001); *Insaniac* (2002); *A Lighter Shade of Pearl* (2002); *The Brown Bunny* (2003); *Defining Reason* (2003); *Inbred Redneck Alien Invasion* (2004); *Joe* (2004); *A Matter of Choice* (2004); *Through a Window* (2005); *The Naked Ape* (2005); *Touching Down* (2005); *Pushing Up Daisies* (2005); and *Stan Kann: The Happiest Man in the World* (2005).

Consider how many movies have "St. Louis" in their titles. Here are some examples: *S.S. St. Louis* (1903); *Vernon Howe Bailey's Sketchbook of St. Louis* (1916); *The St. Louis Kid* (1934); *Visiting St. Louis* (1945); *South of St. Louis* (1949); *Louis in St. Louis* (1992); *Meet Me in St. Louis: The Making of an American Classic* (1994); *The Voyage of the St. Louis* (1995); *Radio Free St. Louis: This is Chuck Norman* (2003); *Little Feat: Highwire Act Live in St. Louis* (2003). And at least three films have been titled *St. Louis Blues* (1929, 1939, and 1958).

Besides those features covered in the foregoing chapters, a number of major productions have been shot at least partially in St. Louis in recent years. Among these are: 1981's *Escape From New York*, with Kurt Russell as the unforgettable Snake Plissken; Chevy Chase's 1983 *National Lampoon's Vacation*, concerning that crazy cross-country trip to Wally World in California (a takeoff on Disneyland); Kevin Costner's 1985 bicycle-racing film, *American Flyers*, with its opening scene at Laclede's Landing; the first Hannibal Lecter film, variously known as *Manhunter* and *Red Dragon: The Pursuit of Hannibal Lecter*, released in 1986; then the more famous Lecter film, *The Silence of the Lambs*, starring Jodie Foster and Anthony Hopkins in their Oscar-winning roles, with a scene shot at Lambert Airport; and *Fever Pitch*, the 2005 baseball flick starring Drew Barrymore in the now-demolished old Busch Stadium.

There are so many films that have St. Louis connections (that are partially set in the city, filmed in the city, have some mention of the city, or feature a major actor from the St. Louis area) that any attempt to quantify them would inevitably fall short. Among the movies on this list are such productions as *The Whirlpool of Destiny* (1916); *The Rebellious Bride* (1919); *Fugitive Lovers* (1934); *Whipsaw* (1935); *The Plainsman* (1936); *Fugitive in the Sky* (1936); *Wells Fargo* (1937); *We Were Dancing* (1942); *Wilson* (1944); *The Naughty Nineties* (1945); *It Happens Every Spring* (1949); *How the West Was Won* (1962); and *The Grave* (2003).

And then there have been many "outstate" productions. Just consider all these films with "Missouri" in their titles: *The James Boys in Missouri*

(1908); *That Boy From Missouri* (1913); *The Girl From Missouri* (1934); *I'm From Missouri* (1939); *In Old Missouri* (1940); *Bad Men of Missouri* (1941); *A Missouri Outlaw* (1941); *Down Missouri Way* (1946); *The World Today: The Man from Missouri* (1946); *The James Brothers of Missouri* (1949); *The Great Missouri Raid* (1951); *Across the Wide Missouri* (1951); *The Missouri Traveler* (1958); *The Missouri Breaks* (1976); *Miss Missouri* (1990); *Mighty Mo: The Battleship USS Missouri* (1998); *Living in Missouri* (2001); and *The Outlaws of Missouri* (2003).

Plus, of course, there have been plenty of movies set in Hannibal, dealing with Mark Twain's two very mischievous boys. I've found a total of 16 films about Huckleberry Finn made between 1920 and 2000, and, as for Tom Sawyer, there are 21 productions dating from 1907 to 2000.

And how about all the films with a strong link to Kansas City? For example: *Chasing Rainbows* (1919); *Lahoma* (1920); *Step on It!* (1922); *Kansas City Princess* (1934); *Sullivan's Travels* (1941); *Whistling in the Dark* (1941); *A Place in the Sun* (1951); *In Cold Blood* (1967); *Casino* (1995); and *Going to Kansas City* (1998). Of course, that's a whole other book.

So, St. Louis and the state of Missouri have been well represented over the past 100-plus years of movie-making. Some have been great and some even classic films, while others were…well, not so great. St. Louis can be proud that it has long been considered the "Gateway to the West." It can be proud that it was home to one of the greatest fairs ever held and that it was the first American city to host the Olympic games. It can also be proud that some of its sons and daughters have gone on to immortality upon the silver screen. And it can likewise be proud of how it has, itself, been represented upon that screen.

Stand tall, St. Louis, realizing that what has made you great aren't just the big things like the 1904 World's Fair and the Olympic Games. The things that make you great are your people and their stories, whether grand and far-reaching, like those depicted in *Meet Me in St. Louis* and *The Spirit of St. Louis*, or simply the tale of one family, as shown in *Parenthood*, or even the story of just two people, as in *White Palace*.

Yes, stand tall, St. Louis, because these films and all the others examined in *Lights…Camera…Arch! St. Louis & the Movies* tell your story to the world!

INDEX

ABOUT THE AUTHOR

Lester Pope (center) with sons Martin and Aaron in 1991.

Lester N. Pope has been a professional writer since the 1960s when he began working as a journalist and his first pieces of fiction were published. He has served on the staffs of publications in five states and currently writes and edits for a monthly magazine, a weekly newspaper, and an online publication. He has received many honors for his writings, including several national awards.

In the non-fiction field, he is known for his celebrity interviews. A few of those he has profiled since the 1960s include civil rights activist Dr. Martin Luther King, Jr., President Jimmy Carter, *Tonight Show* host Jay Leno, former Cherokee Chief Wilma Mankiller, actor/photographer Leonard Nimoy, poet Maya Angelou, baseball Hall-of-Famer Ozzie Smith, former Secretary of State Madeleine Albright, music legends Peter, Paul & Mary, sex therapist Dr. Ruth Westheimer, television personality Willard Scott, former New York Mayor Rudolph Giuliani, music great Ray Charles, and comedians Bob Hope and Bill Cosby.

Many of his works of fiction have been published since 1964. Some of his best known short stories include "Hold Your Nose for America" (published three times under two different titles), "The Only Cure" (conceived and written in draft form when he was 13 and rewritten and published when he was 43), and "The Meek Shall Inherit" (a 23-word-long extra-short-short).

Lester began writing reviews of books and theater for the Louisville *Defender* in 1967 and later started also reviewing motion pictures and television programming. He went on to teach reviewing on the university level. With Bachelors, Masters, and Ph.D. degrees, primarily in communications and journalism, he has served on three university faculties since 1972.

Both of his sons, Martin and Aaron, live in Los Angeles and work as screenwriters.